THE REAL EAST END

The Text by
THOMAS BURKE

The Lithographs by
PEARL BINDER

Copyright © 2013 Read Books Ltd.
This book is copyright and may not be
reproduced or copied in any way without
the express permission of the publisher in writing

British Library Cataloguing-in-Publication Data
A catalogue record for this book is available from the
British Library

Thomas Burke

Thomas Burke was born in Clapham, London in 1886. His father died when he was very young, and at the age of ten he was removed to a home for middle-class boys who were "respectably descended but without adequate means to their support." Burke published his first piece of writing – a short story entitled 'The Bellamy Diamonds' – in 1901, when he was just fifteen. However, proper recognition came in 1916, with the publication of *Limehouse Nights*, a collection of melodramatic short stories set amongst the immigrant population of London's Chinatown. *Limehouse Nights* was serialized in three British periodicals, *The English Review*, *Colour* and *The New Witness*, and received positive attention from reviewers and a number of authors, including H. G. Wells. It also sparked something of a controversy, however, and was initially banned by libraries due to the scandalous interracial relationships it portrayed between Chinese men and white women.

It was these portrayals of London's Chinatown that Burke is best-remembered for. However, there is some degree of confusion over how much of Burke's writing was based in fact; as literary critic Anne Witchard states, most of what we know about Burke's life is based on works that "purport to be autobiographical, yet contain far more invention than truth." Whatever the truth, there is no doubt that, in his day, Burke was regarded as the foremost chronicler of London's Chinatown at the turn-of-the-century. Burke told newspaper journalists that he had "sat at the feet of Chinese philosophers who kept opium dens to learn from the lips that could frame only broken English, the secrets, good and evil, of the mysterious East," and these journalists almost uniformly took him at his word.

Burke continued to use descriptions of urban London life as a focus of his writing throughout his life. Off the back of *Limehouse Nights,* Burke published the thematically similar *Twinkletoes* in 1918, and *More Limehouse Nights* in 1921. However, he was a prolific author who tried his hand at a number of different genres. He semi-regularly published essays on the London environment, including pieces such as 'The Real East End' and 'London in My Times', and during the thirties even tried his hand at horror fiction. Indeed, in 1949, shortly after his death, Burke's short story 'The Hands of Ottermole' was voted the best mystery of all time by critics. Burke also influenced the burgeoning film industry in Hollywood; D W Griffith, for example, used the short story 'The Chink and the Child' from *Limehouse Nights* (1917) as basis for his silent movie, *Broken Blossoms* (1919), and Charlie Chaplin derived 'A Dog's Life' (1918) from the same book.

WATNEY STREET MARKET

BOOKS BY THOMAS BURKE

CITY OF ENCOUNTERS
THE FLOWER OF LIFE
THE SUN IN SPLENDOUR
PLEASANTRIES OF OLD QUONG
THE WIND AND THE RAIN
LIMEHOUSE NIGHTS
THE ENGLISH INN
NIGHTS IN TOWN
THE BOOK OF THE INN

CONTENTS

	PAGE
ITS COLOUR	1
ITS PEOPLE	23
ITS RIVER	88
ITS COMMERCE	126
TAIL-PIECE	161

ILLUSTRATIONS

WATNEY STREET MARKET	*frontispiece*
MIDNIGHT IN LIMEHOUSE CAUSEWAY	*facing page* 17
SPREAD EAGLE YARD, 1931 (*from my studio window*)	23
SPREAD EAGLE YARD, 1932	24
ALDGATE, EVENING	37
JEWISH BURIAL GROUND, BRADY STREET	44
JEWISH BOOKSHOP IN WENTWORTH STREET	50
WEST INDIA DOCK ROAD	62
BLACKWALL TUNNEL	78
ALDERMAN'S STEPS, WAPPING	94
VAULTS (*London Docks*)	98
THE CIRCUS, ALDGATE (*by the Tower*)	104
ST. KATHERINE'S WAY, WAPPING	108
BRICK LANE, BEGEL-SELLER	139
JEWISH RESTAURANT IN BRICK LANE	152
MY LANDLORD, SPREAD EAGLE YARD	161

ITS COLOUR

*E*AST END! ... Visions in the public mind of slums, vice, crime, sin, and unnameable horrors.

East End! ... Dregs of humanity. Beggars and thieves. Bare-footed waifs. Outcasts. Drunkards. Jack the Ripper. Crimping dens. Dangerous streets. Policemen walk in twos and threes. Something worse than Chicago. Sidney Street. Limehouse. Opium dens.

East End! ... Hooligans. Diseased harlots. Public-houses at every corner. Thugs lurking in every alley. Sudden death.

Well, legends are like old soldiers. But old soldiers do eventually fade away, and that is more than legends do. Fact, set beside legend, is a poor, pale thing, apathetic and incompetent to hold its own. Facts fade away and die, but legends are invulnerable and immortal; and the East End legend, I suppose, will last as long as there is any East End. Because the East End did misbehave itself in the forties and fifties of last century, the decent and kindly East End of the twentieth must go on paying for misbehaviour with which it was never concerned. The People are like that; they will cherish their traditions against all truth and all disproof. They will speak of singers as great singers long after the singers' voices have gone to rags. They will applaud once-fine actors who have lost all ability to act. If a man has once had a term of prison he is for ever after an ex-convict. If a man is once charged with a crime and proved innocent, he is remembered for ever as " the man who was charged with——" They love labels and will keep their faith in them long after the print of the label has faded. They will give a politician a good name, or a dog a bad name, and no matter what politician or dog may afterwards do, the label is never changed. So with the East End. They have fastened on the legend and ignored the fact; and if my own early books have had anything to do with nourishing the legend among them, I make no apology. It is their own fault, as I have said elsewhere, for taking imaginative Arabian Nights fictions as though they were newspaper-reporting. I admit to using the East End for my own purposes, and dramatizing it to what I wanted it to be, as many authors have done before and since with the territories of their choice.

The public's muddled notions on the social life of

the East End are accompanied by equally muddled notions on its topography, and even on its location. Many people think that the whole of the East End consists in a district called Limehouse. To a still larger number it means, topographically, any part of London east of a line drawn from Islington to Camberwell, and, sociologically, any quarter where the poor live. You have only to say to these people " slums " and " poor " and " Communism," and they think at once " East End." They do not know that Vauxhall, Camden Town, North Kensington and Battersea are much more truly representative of what they think they mean by the term. Even the Press often goes astray in the matter. My friend, Ernest George, who wrote that moving play, *Down Our Street*, keeps a bookshop in Hackney. Every press paragraph that I have seen about him states that he keeps a bookshop in the East End. In the nineties Arthur Morrison published his *Tales of Mean Streets*, the scene of most of the tales being Hoxton. That book is still described as a book of East End stories. Some time ago I published a tale the scenes of which were Clerkenwell and Kingsland Road. That, too, was reviewed as a tale of East End life.

In truth, the East End is as definite a quarter as the West End. Hammersmith and Notting Hill are West but they are no part of the West End, nor are Edgware Road, or Bayswater, or Paddington, though they are more West than any part of the West End. The East End, then, is only one part of that half of the metropolis which is called East London. The East End itself is the vast

Metropolitan Borough of Stepney. That borough begins at Aldgate Pump and ends at Poplar, with Bethnal Green as its northern boundary and the river as its southern. Within its lines you have all those districts which compose the East End, and their names are Aldgate, Whitechapel (the Ghetto), Spitalfields, Ratcliff, Shadwell, Wapping, Mile End and Limehouse; the Tower Hamlets, in short. This is the true East End, and these are the names which, to the uninformed ear, still carry an odour of misery and evil. But it is, as I say, an odour only, with no substantial source. The East End of Blanchard Jerrold and Doré and James Greenwood perished in their lifetime, and many courts and alleys near the City border, which once were nests of hovels and the haunts of desperadoes, now hold the solid buildings of commerce and industry. Warehouses, wholesale shops, factories, and the offices of small businesses may be found occupying the houses that once were crimping dens and gambling dives. The great god Business has accomplished in a few strokes all those reforms which the philanthropic groups spend many years and tons of other people's money in talking about. If you think you will find here any fruity samples of what is called " low life," I recommend you to look elsewhere—to look off City Road and around the minor streets of certain Midland and Northern and Scottish towns.

None the less, the East End is dramatic. It is peculiarly rich in atmospheres and in variety of human types. It is as respectable as Brixton, but it is not Brixton. It is as well-clothed as Pimlico, but it is not Pimlico. It is right on the edge of the

City; in fact, the City merges into it; but it is not affected by the City. Independent of each other and without warfare, the bleak, brittle life of the City marches with the warm, casual life of the East End. London has many souls, and the East End is its dramatized soul, for it is built of all nations. Its townscapes, if not pleasing, are affecting. All have quick lines of character, for souls from all parts of Europe have wrought this quarter into what it is and have left their impress upon it. Its hundreds of rheumatic courts and alleys, blocked in and left as they were two centuries ago, are charged with exotic atmosphere. Its dusk and its night are apart from the dusk and night of other quarters. Its life may be ugly to those who see modern art as ugly, but, like that art, it is inspired by a gusty strength which comes out in later generations, full but mellow. Its young people are the common plants from which after long breeding our garden flowers come. They take what is; the general tone, though free, is respectable. It has the genuine spirit of Bohemia. It proves what the artists have not yet learnt—that one can lead the Bohemian life, if one wishes to, in strict decency, and that muddle and drunkenness are no necessary part of it. There is no deliberation about this. It does not spring from pose or from poverty. It is the East End's natural way of living. As for poverty, though it can show much of this, you will find deeper poverty in North and South London; and as for drunkenness, you will see much more of that in Shaftesbury Avenue and Jermyn Street than here. If it is crime you want, then again you must look elsewhere. There is to-day no "crime quarter." Crime has become a recognized industry, with depots in all parts of London, and if it flourishes a little more in some parts than in others, those parts are the West and the Far West. Scarcely any of "The Boys" belong to the East End. Study police-court reports for a few days and note the addresses of the smash-and-grabbers, the hold-up men, the car thieves, the burglars. You will note very few East End addresses. There is once in a way a little disorder, created mainly by one small gang, but no more than occurs in any other district. This gang seldom does anything worse than indulge in that kind of outrageous and irritating horseplay common to all spirited and half-grown creatures; and if that kind of thing is to be called Crime, then Oxford and Cambridge are dead-black centres of crime. Such mild disorder as happens is mainly traceable to overcrowding and lack of room-space, which leads to nervous tantrums and the desire to break out. The East End has always been, and I suppose always will be, overcrowded. It is the cheapest quarter of London for living, and it acts as a magnet to the poor of all places. Progress never succeeds in clearing it, for with progress of one class goes retrogression of another. As fast as the younger generation grows up, and makes material progress, and moves to the outer suburbs and rears its children to standards a shade more middle-class, a new host of peasantry from the counties, a new host from the impoverished plains of Europe, and a new set of drifters from other parts of town come in and take their place. And these marry when they are not financially fit for marriage, and set up in one room, and so the overcrowding goes on. But they bear it well, and the horse-play of the one small rough element is rather ebullient than corrosive.

Those comfortable folk who do not cherish the East End legend of violence and depravity cherish one equally unfounded. They link the East End with misery. Misery! There are numbers of places where this may be perceived, but the East End is not one of them. A straight face does not imply personal misery any more than an ever-smiling face implies personal happiness. Yet the legend persists. A week or so ago, a daily-paper gossip-writer, presumably just out of school, described to his readers his adventure of a bus-ride through the East End, and told them that from what he saw he felt that there could be joy in life even (even!) for those who lived in the East End. The acute observer! People of this sort must have got their minds clogged when they were young and never have cleaned them. This attitude to the East End is akin to that attitude which at the words "artist's model" thinks "immorality"; which thinks of Paris as "gay," and dull Antibes, that inferior Torquay, as delightful because the Right People go there; and a walk over the Pyrenees as "romantic" in comparison to a walk over the Pennines. I remember one of our sleekly prosperous West End novelists telling me with a sort of sad despair that after reading some London-byway sketches of mine he felt that it was useless to try to help These People. (He did not call them These People with any *intent* of sneering; he used the term instinctively as a zoologist naming an "order.") He pointed his remark with a personal experience. He had, it appeared, with his natural kindness, ventured out of his West End, and had gone Down There to give assistance at some kind of entertainment, and had found that These People displayed no signs of misery or privation, and expressed no gratitude to him for the sacrifice of his time. When I smiled he seemed unable to perceive where the joke lay. There were actually three jokes.

Another legend is that of the ignorance and illiteracy of the East End people. A brilliant young Cambridge man lately wrote a newspaper article satirizing the working classes as our future rulers, and exposing their ignorance of current affairs. He took his example (of course) from the East End—a Council School boy of fourteen. The article held the usual patronizing tone of the University boy towards the Council School boy; yet this young man must know quite well that ignorance of general matters is not confined to East End boys of fourteen. This ignorance could have been equally well illustrated by scores of examples from among our other "future rulers"—boys of eighteen of his own social rank. If the author thinks all boys of good family are enlightened, and all working-boys dense, any employer can correct him. Again, one of our "intellectual" novelists recorded recently, with a note of wonder, that on his visiting a Whitechapel home the daughters of the house were reading Marcel Proust and a volume of Tchekov's comedies. Why the wonder? Would he have expressed wonder if the same thing had happened in Hampstead? If not, why in this case? Was it due to that ignorance of actual life which is the cause and essence of the intellectuals? Or was it a virtuous presumption that all those who were not lucky enough to be born in "nice" quarters are necessarily witless; that grace and culture are to be expected only in the sons of Balliol? Last year an amiable Divine surprised all informed people by a similar attitude. He announced, with some show, that he had been "Down" to the East End, and had made a discovery. He had discovered that the East End girl washed herself and dressed neatly!

But there are plenty like these people, clotted with half-formed prejudice, and unable to see anything outside their preconceived notions as any part of the real world; always "discovering" things which other people have always known. While the amiable Divine was about his exploring, he might have ventured a little farther into the terrible jungle. He would not then have told the story he did tell of a young girl of to-day, which began with her addressing another girl—"O crikey, 'Arriet . . ." There may be some very aged women in the East End whose name is Harriet, but I will bet the Divine all my cigarette coupons that he can't produce a *young* East End girl of that name, or one who uses the slang of thirty years ago. The names current in the East End to-day are the names current in any other part of London, and the young girls are mainly Joans, Bettys, Viviens, Dorises, Barbaras, Sylvias, and Evelyns. He also put the word "spicy" into the mouth of an East End girl. That again he could not have heard. Any girl of to-day, whether East End or

West End, who wanted to convey what that word used to convey, would use a word borrowed from an American talkie.

The Shadwell or Spitalfields girl is, indeed, no different from any other London girl. You will see her any day in the offices of the City and the shops of the West—bright, pretty, shingled, lipsticked and celanesed; and you will see nothing about her to suggest the awful Shadwell or Spitalfields of your imagination. You may see one type of her in the evenings, setting out from her East End streets, with other girls and young men, all in full evening clothes, for a West End restaurant or a West End dance-hall. And if you exchanged her cheap frocks for the real thing, and put her in the hands of a Bond Street hairdresser, and then set her among a number of the Bright Young Things of Mayfair, the only notable difference would be that the Bright Young Things would have uglier and noisier manners. You may label her " East End Girl " if you like, but the phrase has no more significance than " Clapham Girl " or " Hampstead Girl " or " Wimbledon Girl." If you can perceive anything that does mark her, it is that she

is a little sharper and more common-sensible than her fellows from some other quarters. These virtues are of her streets.

It is the custom in all cities that the rich select for residence the western end of the city, leaving the poor and the strugglers to camp in the east. Something symbolical here, perhaps—the moving process of the suns. Certainly there is a tang of morning about these haggard streets, and their social note, derived from the people, is one of temperate jubilee. The stronger element is the people, and you feel that at any moment this element is likely to wipe the haggard streets from the vision and achieve complete jubilee. Seldom do you see here the frigid, bored faces that you see west of the Royal Exchange. The people are not expressive; their acceptance of life is never vocal, and neither their faces nor their figures are effervescent. It is in the strong, rough-shod tone that you perceive their rich vitality and their gusto for living. They are never tired of life, for they never try to accelerate its tempo. They take it as it comes, and every day is a promise and not a mere repetition of a thousand yesterdays. Watch the crowds coming from the Rivoli or the People's Palace, or from the Palaseum or La Bohème cinemas. Calm faces. Firm pulses. Delight in everyday things. No need of cocktails to whip up energy or interest. No need of the dull prod of freak parties or foolish treasure-hunts. No cold withdrawal from their neighbours. Life has not spoilt their humanity by a blunting variety of interest; they are openly concerned about each other and about you. No outer signs of poverty. They haven't much money, but they do see life, and they keep an appetite for it. The girls, as I say, are marcelled and are dressed in quick copies of Hanover Square —fashion travels even more swiftly than bad news —and the young men are dressed in smart " suitings," perhaps a shade too smart, and have had smart hair-cuts. Only the elderly are dowdy, and many even of these run to furs and Ciro necklaces. There may be no solid background to this outer smartness, but in itself it is a sign of a vitality that is making the tired and overburdened middle classes wonder. Out of this district came the vital minds of H. M. Tomlinson, of Alfred Wolmark, artist, Solomon, pianist, James Rodker, critic, David Bomberg, artist, Noah Elstein and Ernest George, dramatists, Moysheh Oyved, Yiddish poet, Clare Cameron, nature essayist, and Professor Thomas Okey; and more are coming and will continue to come. For further proof of the intelligent impulses that operate here independent of the missionaries, you have only to visit the Bethnal Green and Whitechapel Art exhibitions of the pictures of local working-men. Many of the pictures originally shown there are now in national art collections. The assumption that the East End is peopled by illiterates is dispelled by a brief glance at the facts. The free libraries, of which Stepney alone has four, are always busy; they have nearly 90,000 volumes in constant circulation. Various literary and social circles, composed of young people who support the more popular literary papers, hold regular meetings through the winter season at which some serious writer is the guest, and the People's Palace concerts of chamber music and modern orchestral works are always packed.

Enterprise and genius are born of the mixture of breeds, and in these streets all European races and some Asiatic races have mingled and married outside their race. This bit of London has always been the first bit of London that the poor immigrant saw, and it is the instinct of the wanderer to make his first camp where he lands. So here, in the Tower Hamlets, they camped, meaning to move to the hinterland next week.  But they didn't move, and the camp became a settlement in which they built some shreds of their own country, if only with national musical instruments and national song, and national forms of religious worship. And here they are to-day—Russians, Danes, Jews, Syrians, Egyptians, Armenians, Chinese, Hindoos, Malays, Germans, Roumanians, Swedes and Irish —so mixed and so married that the district is a small America, and the young East End man of to-day may have a Syrian grandfather and an Irish grandmother, and a German Jew for a father. Hence the vitality and the alert perception and the talent.

Its most visible commodities are food, clothes, and jewellery, and these almost give the history of the district. They show the mind of the immigrant, of the wanderer at last ashore. His first thought is for food to maintain strength. Then clothes for warmth. Then jewellery as a handy means of carrying his wealth. Then, when his life is more or less settled, these things assume another proportion; they represent his standing in the community—good feeding, good clothes, and decoration. And so these three commodities become basic commodities and the lowest common measure of success or failure.

I have said that its dusk and its night have a quality of their own, and indeed for me they have. Night, which is everywhere mysterious, is here something more. It is evocative. This may derive from the presence of the river and its long-travelled ships of all countries, or from the fact that more of the old London survives here than elsewhere; or from its peculiar topography. Look at the map and mark how its streets and lanes wander and twist in purposeless convolutions. If the reeling English drunkard made the rolling English road, then the streets and alleys of the East End must have been blazed by a lunatic who had been bitten by Tarantula. Or maybe they were born of the errant footsteps of the first foreign refugees wandering blindly across the marshes for some friendly spot where they might set down their bundles and rest untroubled. However they came, there is no mistaking their effect. The curling alleys, the interlocking courts, the beetling gables and solitary lamps, the blank walls and lakes of silent darkness and the river's black majesty, do create an atmosphere of impending event. Darkness here is true darkness, opulent and velvet. Its beauty is not destroyed, as in the West, by multitudes of arc lamps and glittering night-signs. Lamps, away from the main streets, are few, and night here may be felt in its natural quality. Cities and places are best seen at night. By day a city is engaged in its affairs, but at night it has time to talk to you. And at night vision is restricted to the immediate. One can see only a part, and the part, properly seen, is always greater than the whole. There is no obtrusion of the commonplace whole to distract the attention; there are no clear-cut landmarks of the obvious. There is your visual radius, and beyond that, marked only by melting shadows, the unknown world. At daylight, this unseen and unknown will be merely a mile of Commercial Road or Whitechapel Road or Cambridge Road—explored and known; but at night it is uncharted space in which the part stands out individual and arresting. Within one's little night-bound radius one can truly see the East End; and every corner seems to hold its story.

Fog, too, may be known here in something of its full strength, and in all hues—from white through cobweb grey, yellow and purple to a black more black than darkest night. It has a way of coming suddenly, up from the river, and in a few minutes the aspect and character of the streets are changed, and a rushing multitude of people is transformed into a crawling mass of phantoms. You are going about your affairs at the street's natural pace, and the rhythm of the traffic is at full swell, when, with scarcely a hint of trouble, all honest noise is muted into furtive murmur. The lamps, quickly lit, are no more than glow-worm sparks; human creatures are twisted into shapes of menace; the main streets become sightless gorges, and the shortest alleys stretch into infinitude. Your natural dramatic townscapes have become, in a brief space, melodramatic; and if you wish to know what fog can really be, and the dumb baseless terror it can inspire, you should experience it here. The general night atmosphere of impending event becomes, with fog, impending catastrophe. Darkness is kind, but fog is wicked.

There is the darkness of the riverside, and the darkness of Stepney, the darkness of Limehouse and the darkness of Spitalfields. Each has its quality and its peculiar accompanying life. You may wander about these parts, through the winding and doubling alleys, and see little save varying hues of darkness and lighted windows and shadow falling upon shadow; but you will hear much. You will hear many accents and many tongues and many musics. You will hear gramophones and wireless in Stepney, and the rich Cockney accent. By the river you will hear pianos and concertinas and the hooting of tugs and the ripple of chains. In Limehouse you will hear the liquid accents of Canton and the mournful sound of reed instruments, and in Spitalfields you will hear the guttural Yiddish and old songs of Russia. In the darkness of Stepney you can feel the ordinary London home. By the river you can feel the port and the sea and the sea's wanderers. In the darkness of Limehouse and Spitalfields you can feel the spirit that troubled the air around the waters of Babylon.

As places are better seen at night, so these things are more keenly to be felt at night than at day. Night brings not only cessation of labour, but a

MIDNIGHT IN LIMEHOUSE CAUSEWAY

calm of its own, to which the neighbourhood of the river and the docks lends fluency; and in this calm the elusive spirit of place can rest and make itself known. Side streets and courts are no longer side streets and courts, but great gulfs of Night. Within those gulfs the movements of human creatures cease to be human and become spectral. From out of them come now and then to the keen ear the muffled vibrations of deep experience. Under mist or moonlight these groupings of courts and alleys and straggling streets become sternly beautiful and potent with awe. They have lived long, and have housed their millions. They have known birth and death, love and lust, suffering and joy; they have acquired something from all their creatures, wholesome and sinful, and have given something of themselves. In the bald daytime they are dumb; they are mere rows of houses; only at night do they give some hint of all that they have been and are. But the hint is nothing more than an awareness of the ache of life; that ache which is with us in pleasure as in pain, and which here is the ache of simple poor people living out simple lives as workers, wanderers, exiles and housewives. In this dramatic country and under this brooding darkness they sleep, each kind with its separate dream, and give the night a more poignant quality than the night of any other London quarter knows. Midnight darkness here is charged with everything of the strange and the awesome. It is useless to tell yourself that these alleys are inhabited by quiet, simple, working people, who have to be abed in order to be at work at six o'clock in the morning. Your skin knows better. They are inhabited by all man's desires and thronged with whispers. There is melancholy in the fall of a shadow; grief in the single pale gas-gleam which makes the darkness more awful than utter darkness. The spell of grue is upon you, and you know again the night-fears of childhood.

Nothing, I think, has held a larger place in my imaginative life than this country. I love other parts of London more, but the East End, for me, has always been all cities crystallized. Long before I knew it, it was part of my mind. When I was seven years old, and attending my first school, I sat beneath a large-scale wall-map of London, and even then the place-names—Ratcliff, Isle of Dogs, Shadwell, Limehouse, Spitalfields—fascinated me, as Trebizond and Samarkand fascinate others; and the street-names ran in my mind like a recondite rune. I would repeat them to myself in bed—Goodman's Stile, Gracie's Alley, Sweet Lilac Walk, West India Dock Road, Amoy Place, Juniper Street, The North-East Passage, Kent and Essex Yard, Salmon Lane, Cinnamon Street, Coverley Fields, Ropemaker's Fields, Oriental Street, Cuba Street, Frying-Pan Alley, Elbow Lane, Green Bank, Maize Row, Cotter's Green, Drood Yard, Flower-and-Dean Street, Folly Wall, Blue Anchor Fields, Island Row, Three Colt Street, Havanna Street, Canton Street, Mutton Walk, Houndsditch, Drum Yard, Irish Court, Malabar Street, Silver Street, Gold Street, Assam Street, Manilla Street, Ocean Street, Cadiz Street, Glasshouse Fields, Tobago Street, Wapping Wall. Though I had never seen them I knew these streets in dreadful dreams and pleasant imaginings. In sleep, I met lovely sweethearts in Flower-and-Dean Street. I had heart-tearing escapes in Drood Yard, and dare-devil adventures in Frying-Pan Alley. Nightmares brought me hideous minutes in Elbow Lane, and in Gracie's Alley I played the heroic saviour. When, later, while still a child, I made actual acquaintance with Spitalfields and Shadwell, they became the setting of my earliest and most ardent experiences. So much so that if ever, far away from London, I think unwittingly of London, it is those winding streets and clotted courts that I see and those meagre companies of lamps. I first saw them with the eyes of boyhood and only at night; thus they made an impression which twenty years of daylight acquaintance have not been able to eradicate. There, for the first time in my life, a girl turned at a corner and smiled at me, a drunken man at an upper window roared at me. There I first realized the magic of a street organ playing in the darkness. There I saw Rabbis, and for the first time saw foreigners from distant lands, and there I first felt the poetry of lamplight and the splendour of ships and the greatness of rivers. In time it became for me a land where stories could be picked from the air, or snatched, as I have said, at every corner. In the crowding and various life of this quarter, they grow in dozens, where the stereotyped life of "better-class" districts yields scarcely one. And they should, for all the folk tales of all the seven seas have been carried here and told upon the evening air; tales of Russia and Roumania and Palestine; tales of India; tales of Scandinavia, tales of Cathay, tales of ships and storms, and tales of London and of the English countryside.

And tales are still to be gathered here, though they seldom appear in the local Press. They are not to be gathered by busy news-gatherers. They await the idle ear. Every ship has its news, no longer strange, perhaps, but still news; news of things seen in other cities and of the events of the passage. In the inner parts, around Whitechapel, there are foreigners with whispered news of how they entered London without passport. In the coffee-shops and lodging-houses there are newcomers with tales of Russia and of Poland and Germany, and of the domestic or economic disaster which led them to pack up and seek new fortune in London. There are men in hiding. There are tales to be heard from aged Cockneys who have seen Stepney grow to what it is, and who knew the Highway when it was what it was. There are old men with tales of sailing-ship days which they will tell in their cottages whose front rooms are massed with tenderly carved models of ships and pictures of ships. There are tales to be heard in the Ghetto, in rooms dressed with the emblems of Judea, of the many wanderings that led the family at last to London; and tales to be heard of families that came from the farms of Norfolk and Lincolnshire and Suffolk, and made their first home here, with hope of better things that never reached the happy terminus of fact. And there are the daily stories, to be heard at every door, of how the hard times are being met.

All these tales the casual wanderer of the right sort may gather in passing. In the streets and the shops and the restaurants, he may have much good talk, for, as I have said, the true Bohemian spirit operates here. There is no hesitation or withdrawal, nor that cold repetition of parrot-phrases by which the standardized Englishman fences with the stranger until he proves him an equal, the sort of man one can introduce. Talk, once opened, is free and personal; unbosomed; and I, for one, find this talk, in its way, a good balance to talk with the polite. It is talk based on reality and on the immediate experience of those who live close to the elemental things. In mean streets people have to live singly, not play at living with the support of supers. They have to get down to life, not walk on its edge. Hence, mean streets hold a variety lacking in the noble streets. The noble streets, being noble, are mostly reticent. But the mean streets, filled by creatures who see life straight and live it straight, instead of through a wadding of book-culture, have a thousand points of interest.

Not that the East End is without its noble street. It has one that can stand comparison with any of the great London highways, and one that is full of common interest. This is the Whitechapel Road and Mile End Road, the great Roman highway which runs to-day, as it did centuries ago, straight into London from the Roman settlement at Colchester. It is as broad as the entrance to a great metropolis should be, and it puts to shame the poor pinched entrances at the centre of town of the Dover Road, the Brighton Road, and even the Great North Road. For the greater part of its length, it is lined with trees. Its story deserves a volume to itself; indeed, the story only of that section between Stratford and the City calls for a historian. It was one of the earliest roads into London, and while many of its contemporaries have been supplanted, and have disappeared or become grass-grown tracks dimly perceived on the outskirts, its traffic, from its first years, has never eased. An echo of its past importance may be found in the number of Yards which were once the yards of inns. Most of the inns have vanished, but the yards remain; in several of them the bedroom galleries may still be seen, and in one of them the coach office still stands. The best example is Nag's Head Yard.

Thick as its life was, it goes on to-day thicker than ever, full of importance and yet with time for the little intimate things of every day. For a secondary highway, there is Commercial Road East, the Tilbury road. This has not the dignity of Mile End Road, but it is an important road for London. It is a road from many docks, and along it comes much of the material that supports the life and the industries of the greatest old city of the world.

These two roads, converging and meeting Leman Street and Commercial Street at Gardiner's Corner, one of the busiest junctions of all London, make two major veins through the body of this quarter; and from them goes all the life that feeds the ramification of hamlets and streets which have grown out of them and which make what we call The East End. One may say of them, with more truth than of Mona Lisa's head, that upon them all the ends of the world are come.

SPREAD EAGLE YARD, 1931 *from my studio window*

ITS PEOPLE

IT is in one of the old Yards that Pearl Binder has made her home, and she has chosen well. She enjoys a rural atmosphere in the centre of the town. Her cottage windows face directly on to a barn filled with hay-wains and fragrant with hay, and a stable, complete with clock and weather-vane; and they give a view of the metropolitan life of Whitechapel. One realizes here how small London still is, how close it still is to the fields and farms of Essex and Cambridgeshire. All about the district one finds rustic touches conflicting with the urban and the maritime. Horses are still important here—there are many stables and forage contractors—and cattle are often to be seen in progress along its roads. Shoeing-forges are still to be seen and the ring of hammer on anvil still to be heard. Pearl Binder's yard has retained more of its rural characteristics than most, and the situation of her cottage, near the mouth of the Yard, gives her the best of both worlds. When one is tired of looking at the hay-wains and the pigeons and the sparrows and the horses, one can look obliquely from its windows and study the news-reel of the streets.[1]

[1] Since the above was written the venerable Yard has become a Luna Park Fun Fair, complete with mutoscopes, ghost-trains, darts, rifle-range, and wiggle-woggle. By the time this book is in the book-shops it may have become a garage, an auction-mart, or once again a hay-yard.

Upon an evening of early October I spent a couple of hours at those windows, and saw almost as much life pass across the little segment of the street which the angle of the archway disclosed as I would have seen in the street itself. Through this loop-hole of retreat, indeed, I could catch really more of the spirit of the place than from the thick of the traffic, since everything that passed across it was momentarily arrested and isolated before being absorbed into the invisible commerce from which it had come and into which it went. I saw, clearly and singly, pale faces from the back courts and salt-red faces from the sea; tawny faces from Middle Europe, olive faces of Jewish children, dark brown faces from the East, and the sallow face of the healthy Cockney. They came rushing; they were focussed; they rushed on. A torrent of faces, each drop of which had its moment of inertia. An orchestra of footfalls, each one of which paused to register its tone in the Yard. A kaleidoscope of racing legs, each one of which was held in slow-motion by the given point across which it raced. I saw the suave gleam of lighted tramcars and the yellow streak of high-powered runabouts. I saw the flash of white legs in socks, the deliberate jungle tread of canvas trousers, the flicker of silk stockings and the passage of hobnail boots. I saw legs for the first time as legs only. I saw fat legs, slim legs, wooden legs, distorted legs, and legs that I only knew were legs because they were attached to human bodies. I saw the dark proud heads of young Jewesses, whose beauty seldom survives the fifteenth year, and the sharp bright prettiness of

SPREAD EAGLE YARD, 1932

the little Cockney blondes which survives everything but marriage. And I saw the veritable Wandering Jew. He passed across that rough triangle, complete with long staff, and clad in the rags of all nations and all ranks. He had, no doubt, been poor in seven European countries and twenty European towns; in mountain passes and valley villages; in the slums of Cracow and under the beaming skies of the Mediterranean. And directly behind him came an old woman whom I knew, an old woman who had been poor for sixty years in one street of the East End.

I saw silken waists with serge arms about them. I saw the shuffling but unhesitating feet, and the beating stick, of the blind matchseller. I saw the steady rhythmic swing of blue trousers and big boots. I saw a black-haired angel-boy out of a Murillo canvas selling the Jewish *Evening News*. I saw two negro children with golliwog heads. I saw a Jewish bookmaker take a stand up the Yard and settle with his clients. They came singly, with hasty back-glances—shopkeepers, labourers, young women, old women, girls, boys, Jews and Gentiles, from well-dressed, through the shabby, to rags. They came in expectant cheerfulness and they went away in realized cheerfulness. Most of them made the motion of spitting on the coins they received. I saw an elderly Chinese wearing mountain-climbing boots, a captain's cap, a steward's jacket and corduroy trousers. I saw one of the most serenely beautiful faces I have seen in my waking life, and some as ugly as the faces of the " social leaders " in the illustrated weeklies. I saw Malays in blue dungarees and flaming scarves. I smelt hay and petrol and cavendish and woodbine and cigar. I smelt garlic and fur and wool. I smelt malt and roast beef and fish and chips. I smelt sandal-wood and that sharp smell which the Englishman finds in the black. I heard heavy feet and light feet and slouching feet. I heard the grinding of gears and the purr of cars and the racket of trams crossing points. I heard voices of every timbre and every accent. I heard chatter and giggle, complaint and jabber and cry, in five languages. Some voices bubbled, some squeaked, some rasped; some were not voices but coughs, and some were as light and frail as snowflakes. All this sound and stir, as it entered the Yard, blended into one deep, rich, 'cello surge of life. The Second Movement of the " Pathetic " could have found its inspiration there.

Watching that archway, and the life that moved across it, I was able to guess the time of the evening. From a Birnam Wood of legs it became, slowly, a plain—a G. P. R. James plain, crossed by solitary travellers. When it was Birnam Wood, I knew that the clock was between six and seven. When it was a mere thicket I knew that the clock was between seven and eight. When it became the G. P. R. James plain, I knew that eight was past. When it was once again a Birnam Wood I knew that nine o'clock was come, and I went out into the October evening.

In the fashionable world October is the month for the country, for huntin' and shootin', but for my part it is the month for town. The October evenings, when, under a smudge of bronze sunset, the street lamps and the coloured windows of the shops make their autumn debut with a green dusk, and the people reflect something of the zest and bite of this season, are, for me, an annual excitement. Autumn's awakening is as significant for human creatures as spring's awakening is for the creatures of the wild. It may be the time of Nature's decay, but for mankind it seems to be a time of rejuvenation, when they wake up from the languor of summer and turn towards the mental activity of winter. In this district it is a sort of opening of the year. The cinemas again begin to receive crowds. Ices are " out " and roast chestnuts are " in "; also winkles and whelks. The little newspaper shops begin to display Chinese masks and crackers in anticipation of Guy Fawkes Day. Whist-drives are organized, cricket clubs and tennis clubs give their end-of-season dances, and grocers and butchers and public-houses announce that their Christmas Clubs have " commenced," and altruistically invite their customers to Pay What You Like and Have What You Like. (One or two, who have made unhappy discovery of the legal interpretation of the phrase, have the sense to add to the invitation " —to the Value of your Money ".) Evening Classes begin their Winter Sessions for such studies as Horology, Applied Optics, Stone Masonry and Brass Finishing, Woodwork and Drawing, as well as the

more intellectual studies; and the officials of the Bands of Hope, the mothers' missions and the young people's leagues canvass so zealously for converts that one might almost think they were insurance agents on a handsome commission basis. Most Octobral is the muffin-man's bell, which announces the beginning of autumn as the lavender-woman's cry announces the end of summer. In other parts of London these two cries are the only cries that survive to-day out of Wheatley's London Cries, but eastward, besides hay-wains and the rural atmosphere, many touches of the past survive. There is the old lady who sits on doorsteps and mends cane chairs. She travels with a bundle of straw-plait, and announces her business in a long-drawn cry of the early eighteenth century: "Any cane cha-a-airs to me-en-end?" There is the man who hawks those long red cylinders which our grandmothers carefully fixed over window-ledges and under doors, in order to keep out any possible threat of fresh air: "Buy any sa-an-and bag? Buy a *win*-der bag?" Children still build here the grotto—bits of stone and brick, with a flower or so and an inch of lighted candle—"Please remember the grotter"—and haven't the least idea that they are honouring St. James of Compostella and the pilgrim's scallop-shell. Men and girls who, but for change of costume, might have stepped out of the Wheatley prints, still carry round feather mops and brooms, and still cry cherries and strawberries from door to door. Once or twice I have seen a ghostly hansom, turning from some ghostly stable in Whitechapel Road, and carrying the music of his ghost bells into the city; and in Cambridge

Road I was jerked back to the last years of Victoria by the sight of a man with a small barrow and—the musical glasses. So much of the old survives that I wish room could be found for one of the few old things that I really miss—the baked-potato can. Often, on a winter's night, I have seen the glow of a street-corner stove, and have hurried hopefully towards it, only to find the indigestible roast chestnut. When I have inquired about the disappearance of the baked potato, whose merchants used to cry the cheering legend of " Warm yer 'ands and fill yer belly for a penny ! " I have always received the same story. " Nothing in baked taters now. They were killed by the fish-and-chip places. Chips is easier to eat in the street than a baked potato. All the youngsters prefer a paperful of chips. Or chestnuts."

Another institution that has disappeared from these streets is the music hall. In the past it had many—the Paragon, at Mile End; the Cambridge in Commercial Street (which Charles Chaplin, when I showed it to him, remembered playing in); the Poplar Hippodrome; and the Foresters. Their frames are still to be seen, but the red nose and the rich noise are no more part of them. (The Cambridge is now a tobacco warehouse !) To-day its nearest is just over its border—the " London," at Shoreditch, where the genuine Cockney music hall still breathes and flourishes. I have no interest in the theatre, with its dull plays about that little thimbleful of the people which has butlers and country houses and French maids (playwrights never seem to meet anybody with less than £10,000 a year); but the music hall is a thing apart. It is an amalgam of all the world's grotesquerie, and in its very idiocy it is legitimate. The music hall performer, too, needs so much more skill, so much more personality than the theatre performer. He has no Shaws or Somerset Maughams or Pirandellos or Tchekovs to write his lines for him. He has to work upon stuff written either by himself or by obscure people living in the back-streets of the near suburbs. And he has no support. The actor always has one, and often three or four, persons on the stage with him, making a background for his part; the music hall performer is alone. Actors have the whole evening in which to make an impression; the music hall man has fifteen or twenty minutes, and he must get attention within a few seconds of his entrance or fail. How few, even of the approved actors, can stand alone on the stage and hold the attention of a full house even for one minute. Yet music hall men can hold a house merely by looking at it. If you want to see good and effective acting, it is to the music hall, not the theatre, that you must go.

At the "London" you will still find a memory of the gusto and bouquet that marked the music hall in its best days—the late nineties. The world of music hall is a world ruled by its own peculiar insanity. It is a world beyond the edges of our seven seas, a widdershins world full of Mad Toms of Bedlam and furious fancies. Nothing happens in that world as it happens with us; disaster lurks not only here and there but everywhere. If they describe a wedding which they have attended it is like no wedding that we know. If they present you with a conjuring act, they feel that a conjuring act by itself is not sufficient value, so they wear some marked but entirely incongruous costume for it— that of Cossacks or Tibetans or Eastern potentates or midshipmen. If they sing a comic song about a Scoutmaster they present you with such a Scoutmaster as none has seen outside dreams; to the mad character they add a madness of clothes and a madness of incident and  episode. It is a world beyond even planetary distance of this world, or the theatre world, or the film world. A world utterly grotesque yet convincing. Not the world of a Midsummer Night's Dream, nor the world of Caliban, but such a world as the august Comic Spirit might perceive after too many welsh rarebits. It is in being still at the Holborn Empire and the Victoria Palace, in central London, and full of breath at the Shoreditch "London."

Performers and audience here make a whole. The audience know the performers, and the performers know the "London" audience, and realize that it demands differential treatment from that given to the Holborn audience or the Victoria Palace audience. It is a rough-friendly audience. I once saw a demonstration of its inner character when it gave a clear and peremptory "bird" to a woman singer who refused to recognize "birds" of any kind. She was not incompetent, but to some extent she had earned their dislike by giving them a song that was a season old and had grown stale in all ears. After the first verse she was greeted with that monotonous and rhythmic clap-clap-clap, clap-clap-clap. She went steadily through the chorus, and on to the second verse. To the clap-clap-clap succeeded a stamping of boots. She ignored it. Then came noises registering disgust. She ignored them. She went to the third verse and chorus. Then came the sing-song command: "Get-off, get-off . . . get-off, get-off." Her mouth by now had a strained set, and her eyes were hard, but she did not obey the command. Even when she had finished the final chorus, and might with dignity have got off, she did not get off. The stage was blacked out, save for a single spot-light, and she went on to the dance which followed the song; a dance to the same stale air. She cut no second of her performance, but went steadily through the dance to a growing riot of expressed unpopularity—claps, get-offs, noises, laughs and stamps—until she came to the legitimate end of her act and danced off with a farewell wave. Once she was able to get off, I thought, she would keep off. But no. With superb nerve she came back to face the hostile house and to bow; and the house honoured itself. It had no sympathy for bad performers, but it recognized courage and audacity and endurance. On the last chord of her music the noises ceased and the get-offs ceased, and the claps and stamps changed their note. Her return was greeted with such a storm of honest claps and stamps and such a hurricane of those piercing friendly whistles which used to be the superlative of popular applause, that those behind who had not seen the act must have thought that a new star had arisen. She was, I think, the worst turn in the bill, and her pluck got her the biggest " hand." In a more staid house she would have received frozen silence and worse—no re-booking.

Why the East End proper has allowed its music halls to pass I do not know. But not only has it allowed these to pass; it has allowed an even more East End feature to pass. Premierland, the home of East London boxing, is closed. So much does boxing mean to the East End that it might almost be classed as a local industry. Hundreds of lads are attracted to it, scores are engaged in it, and there is a never-failing supply of novices, and a never-failing audience for any display. Such heroes are those who achieve distinction in it that Ministers and Members might look with dismay on the magnificent reception accorded to a victor on returning to his home-street. To witness the return of one of the local stars of boxing (at the time of writing they are Kid Berg, Teddy Baldock, and Dick Corbett) would make a film star really ill. And yet Premierland is closed.

This, on Sunday afternoons, was one of the sights of London. Contests were held on Monday and Thursday nights also, but as a spectacle the Sunday afternoons were unique. Many people thought that it must be a rough-house; much rougher, that is, than the ordinary boxing-hall, because it was in the East End. But it was not. It was a little more vocal than the Ring or the Albert Hall; a little more thoughtless in its language; but not rough. On that side it was well served by the attendants, most of whom were or had been boxers. I have spent many a Pleasant Sunday Afternoon there—boxing and music are all that London offers to fill its aching Sunday afternoons—and I regret its passing. I am no connoisseur of boxing, but I liked the crowd and the beautiful movements of the trained bodies of the young men in the ring. Experts went there to see boxing—and sometimes saw it. The bulk of the crowd went to see fighting—and often saw it. I went to see a ballet which, to me, was more beautiful than any formal stage ballet. When the arc-lights over the ring went up, the hall was no longer a hall but a scene out of Hogarth or Goya. The lights cut the hall horizontally in two, and made a knife-edge between the smoky gloom of the tiers of seats and the blaze of the floor. The tiers became a violet circle spotted with pale dabs which were faces. Before the show began these faces were coarse and towzled; once it was in progress they became elemental. Boys wandered about the rows of seats calling "Ices!" and "Fine orange!" The thing opened with no parade. The referee would appear from some obscure hiding-place, and take a raised seat at the ring-side. The time-keeper would follow him. Two or three stout fellows in sweaters would appear with pails. And then the M.C. would climb through the ropes and take the centre of the ring, and the thing would be on. With his appearance the babble was suddenly arrested. He would lift an arm with air of prelude to a mighty drama. In the tones of a town-crier he would announce forthcoming events, and then turn to the business of the afternoon. With an air of weary tolerance he would announce the first event, knowing that nobody was interested in first events. Out of a dark hole would come the victims and their seconds. In street-clothes these victims appeared as ungainly as most boys of their age, but under the arc-lights, stripped to a pair of shorts, they were seen in all their animal grace, and their bodies lent them a personality denied by their heavy pink faces and slack jaws. They were alert and clean. They passed through the crowd like running water over a muddy river-bed. Their seconds would gather about them, giving perfunctory advice with a sort of good-natured contempt. They were only kids; nobody had come to see *them*; they were there merely to fill up the bill. They created more amusement than interest. The M.C. would introduce them with a bawl. " Order there ! Silence ! " Then, syllable by syllable—" Nine-stone *contest* of six two-minute *rounds* between Moggy *Keeks*, Cradley Heath, and Bill *Fishfork*, Rotherhithe. On my r-right— KEEKS. On my l-left—FISHFORK." There would be a spot of applause. The boys would bob awkwardly in acknowledgment. The M.C. would leave the ring. The time-keeper would bark " Seconds *out* ! " the bell would go and the boys spring from their seats. For some seconds you would hear nothing but the thud of soft feet and the pad-pad of glove on body. Their faces were intent, their eyes wary, their lips set in half-smiles. Their limbs were wire and lightning. They appeared to know neither cruelty nor mercy. The silence never lasted long. It was broken either by a skilful blow or a mighty swipe, or by the absence of either. The crowd demanded fistic action, but for me the panther movements and the beautiful momentary poses were sufficient. Every good blow received recognition from one section and every slogging mix-up received it from another section. If nothing happened in the first few seconds a voice would float out of the violet cloud above: " Come on, there! Come on. Show us something." Other voices, having been started by a Leader, formed a Chorus. " Use that left. Come on, Bill. Come on. Now! Now you got him." At first these voices would be conversational; and the M.C.'s monotonous " Keep quiet, there!" could still be heard. But once one of the boys had started something, the voices merged in a roar, and the M.C. would give up. As usual with beginners there was more fighting than boxing, and soon both bodies would be marked with red patches and both faces with bruises. By the way they went at it, one would think that they were settling a private quarrel, and really wanted to hurt each other; but the moment the bell went they would drop hands in the middle of a blow, and trot to their corners like children returning from play. So it would go on, round by round to the end, unless the referee stopped it, as he often did in those early events where one lad was hopelessly outclassed or where neither was really trying. Event would follow event up to the middle of the afternoon, when " the big 'un " was staged—a fifteen or twenty-round affair. This was what the crowd had come to see, and this indeed moved them. The violet cloud would

ALDGATE

Evening

come to life, with heads wagging and bobbing. A vicious blow, well landed, would bring from it a sharp, concerted " Ugh ! " Some of the company would get so wrought up, that they took a mimic part in the fight; they sat with clenched fists, delivering each blow in miniature and retreating from its answer. To sit in front of one of these enthusiasts was not comfortable. As the fight drew near the distance, so the clamour increased. The place became a roaring, steaming maelstrom with, in its centre, one firm little island of silence and sense—the ring. There, untouched by the fury about them, the two white figures would steadily and quietly box on, in pursuit of their job of providing a Pleasant Sunday Afternoon.

But the East End streets themselves are of more abiding appeal than any theatre or cinema, or even than the glorious lunacy of the music hall or the hot, concentrated parable of Premierland. I can wander for hours about them, or sit for hours in a café window, and am never fatigued and never left with an empty minute. One of my favourite spots is an upstairs window-table at a little tea-shop at Aldgate, alongside Butcher Row, with a corner view of the High Street. So thick and various is the panorama, and so continuous, that if it were not so well-balanced in interest, half an hour of it would give one visual indigestion. City and East End meet here, and between five and six o'clock it is a tempest of people. Not only is it a strait between the two districts ; but the section outside the Three Nuns Hotel is the lounging place or outdoor club. At summer mornings and all evenings you will see groups of men standing about there, young and old, prosperous and so-so, but none of them in rags or exhibiting any sign of woe. At all hours they present a scene of idle busy-ness. What they do there, besides gossip, I do not know. They have no air of being unemployed; yet they have no air of having any work to do. They do not appear to pass betting slips and they do not lounge in the alert-furtive way that marks the crook keeping an appointment with some of the " boys " or the hand-bag man with an eye on the buses. They just stand and talk. They do not even lean against the pillars of the Underground station; they just stand upright in the middle of the pavement. When this lounging crowd receives the home-going crowd from both east and west, you can picture the tempest. This point is a bus-stop, a char-à-banc stop, and a tram terminus; and if you shift your glance from the window for half a minute, you are sure to miss some interesting touch of human behaviour. Pavements and roadway offer a dish of all-sorts. All classes and all races are to be observed. You have the Rolls-Royce gliding into Essex and the second-hand two-seater spitting its way to East Ham. You have the little factory-girl and the superior typist. You have the Jew fur-dealer and the shipping clerk. You have the shabby man with his own thriving business and the smart young man who is somebody's slave. You have newsboys, banana merchants, Rabbis, negroes, pedlars, pretty girls, old women, dockers, sailors, Albanian gipsies, and office-boys. And all, save the loungers by the

Three Nuns, are in motion—some strolling, some walking, some running, and the rest fighting for places on trams and buses and envying the office-boys who go home free by stealing rides on the backs of lorries.

This tea-shop was for something more than a year a regular club of mine, and I came to know many of the faces there. The company was as well assorted as the populace of the streets. Jews, sailors, shop assistants, clerks, mothers with children, and country people waiting for the Brentwood and Chelmsford long-distance coach. Most of my attention I gave to the other side of the window, but I did sometimes look round the long room, and after many visits I began to be interested in a girl who was a regular customer at a regular hour, and always sat at a particular table. A table well away from the window. She appeared to find no pleasure in the window-spectacle, and no pleasure in anything else. She took her tea and looked at nobody. What attracted me to her was her pearly and unearthly pallor. It seemed against all the laws of medicine that a girl with such a dead-white face could be alive and move. It was not a tragic face or a miserable face or a sick face; it was a face of beautiful outline expressing nothing, and but for its extraordinary pallor I would not have noticed her. But that pallor fascinated me. At first I thought that she had overdone the *poudre de riz*, but at a closer glance I saw that she was innocent of any make-up. It was a natural pallor. Looking at her was like looking at Death. And as a symbol of Death, Death robbed of the grim aspects that poets have allowed it, Death gentle and benign, she was perfect. She was so pale that to myself I named her the Snow Maiden, and so young that the pathos of her case used to touch me. It was clear that she would not be taking tea for long (another year, I thought) and it was clear that she had known little of the gaieties and the delight in life that healthy girls know. In the course of a few months she seemed to grow yet paler, and her face lost even the thin lustre it once had had. She would walk listlessly to her table, give her order without raising her head, and, when her tea came, take it with eyes fixed distantly on a spot of the table. At the end of eight months her face was so white that the aprons of the waitresses, even allowing for the fact that they were not snow-white, looked like mud against that face. I felt an ache of the heart every time I glanced at her. I wanted to talk to her and do something about it. I felt that she ought not to be where she was: London was clearly hastening the end. She ought to be in the country or by the sea. There, she might know a little health and might postpone for a year or two the obvious end; but in Aldgate she had no chance. I felt furious with life that it should compel her to remain in Aldgate, working, no doubt, in a crowded and ill-ventilated workroom. On a few odd occasions when I was looking at her, she looked up and her eyes met mine, and in the fraction of a second, which was the full time of that meeting of glances, those eyes held such dumb, unconscious appeal that I felt I must there and then sell everything I had, if by doing so I could comfort her or restore her to health. But I had no chance of doing that or even of speaking to her. In that fraction of a second when she realized that her eyes were meeting mine, and that I was returning interest and sympathy in my glance, she looked away and frowned, and thereafter stared at the table and communed with her own affairs.

A little later, her visits were interrupted. She had always been a regular visitor—that is, whenever I was there she was there—but towards the end of the year, often, when I went there, she was not there. Sometimes she was, and sometimes she wasn't; but when she was there her face had become so strikingly white that even regular customers gave her a second glance. More than once she appeared to be on the verge of fainting. As the year went on her visits became less and less frequent, and I saw her slowly fading away. I could see that tailors' work-room in which I fancied she worked, and I could see the back-street home—cramped conditions, bad drains, three sleeping in a room, poor food, and, no doubt, overwork—all hastening the end which they had created. Her face haunted me long after I was away from Aldgate, and often, when I found that she did not appear for tea, I was glad; the sight of her gave me such pain and anger.

There came a time when, in the space of ten weeks (I took tea there three times a week) she had not once appeared; and I knew then that I should never see her again.

I never did see her again. But I had news of her. There was a girl, an equally regular customer, who often sat at that table, and I summoned the courage to approach her and ask if she knew what had been the fate of the poor failing child.

"Who? Oh—*her*. On the films now."

"On the films? Poor child.... She looked to be dying when she was here. I should think that work would finish her."

"*Dying?* Finish her? Finish *her?* Why, she's as strong as a horse, that girl. I bet she's fitter than either of the waitresses. Her dying? You make me laugh. No, she's on the films and doing well. Her face makes people think she's got one foot in the grave, but she's stronger than me. It was her face got her where she is. Somebody on the films saw her in the office, and she was just the type they wanted. They got a small part for a consumptive girl, and she was just It. She made such a hit with it—though she didn't do anything except what they told her to do; if she was a hen she wouldn't have enough brains to run out of the way of a motor—yes, she made such a hit they've written a special story round her. She's to be a new kind of Vamp—a palè, kiss-me-before-we-gather-at-the-river sort of Vamp. She don't have to set herself at the man in the story. And she don't have to be cute. She just has to be herself and do just like she always did wherever she was—in the office or here. Getting what she wants without knowing it, just with those dying-child eyes and the galloping-consumption face. Getting a nice screw, too. She's got a car already on the strength of it."

My annoyance at being "had" by life was a little tempered by the knowledge that I had assisted in the making of a film-star. Remembering those glances, I could count myself as the first victim, the practice model, of the new-style, dying-child Vamp.

I have said that the East End is the camping-ground of the immigrant, and it always was. It seems as though London quite early set this quarter aside for them. The invasion began as far back as 1686, when Huguenot immigrants, under the revocation of the Edict of Nantes, fled their own country, reached London and settled in Spitalfields. For some time Spitalfields was then as much a French colony as Old Compton Street, Soho, is to-day. It was from these French immigrants that Spitalfields took up and developed the silk-weaving industry for which it was, up to the early nineteenth century, famous throughout England. Later, in 1708, arrived two thousand German immigrants whose territory had been invaded and spoiled by the French. They camped in what is now White Horse Lane, Stepney, where they were fed and clothed by the London people until, by a public subscription of some thousands of pounds, arrangements were made to distribute them to different parts of the country. The settlement of the Chinese and other Eastern immigrants dates from the late eighteenth and early nineteenth century, when the great docks were built and trade with the East began to expand. The Scandinavians began to arrive about the same time, but they have now shifted their quarters across the river to Rotherhithe. The Russians and Poles came most thickly in the eighties and nineties.

The Jews have been settled in London since the twelfth century, and their earliest settlement is recorded in two street-names—Old Jewry and Jewry Street, close to which is the Great Synagogue of London. But in 1290 they were banished and were not seen again until Cromwell lifted the ban and permitted them to return. The second colony was formed in this district in the early eighteenth century, and there is in Mile End Road a Home for Aged Jews bearing a tablet giving its history. It was originally a hospital for poor Jews, and near it was established in 1747 the first of many Jewish burial-grounds—for Spanish and Portuguese Jews. But it was not until the early nineteenth century that they came in real numbers and founded a Ghetto. The Spanish and Portuguese Jews died out, or were absorbed as Englishmen, and their place was taken by German Jews, Polish Jews, Russian Jews, Roumanian Jews, Bulgarian Jews—Jews from every country where the Law of the Pale still held, fleeing from intermittent persecution to the one country where nothing was asked them save good behaviour, and where the law operated for them as it operated for the natives. But there will be no further immigration of homeless foreign Jews. That has been stopped, and it seems that all future Jews of the East End will be English-born Jews. Whether they chose Whitechapel because it was already the resting-place of fleeing aliens, or whether there was some divine plan behind a blind choice, one cannot say. But it is curious that the parish church of Whitechapel, which stands almost in the centre of the Ghetto, has borne, from the *fourteenth century*, the name of St. Mary Matfelon, a word based on the Hebrew word

JEWISH BURIAL GROUND, BRADY STREET

"matfel," a woman delivered of a son. The presence around it of thousands of Israel's sons points both its Hebrew name and that name's significance.

I visited the other day a house in Whitechapel which in years to come may be given a plaque. In that house a girl friend of Miss Binder's, the artist of this book, spent her childhood. The family were poor, and had but two rooms, and the girl, when she was five years old, slept in a small bed in the corner of the living-room. She was put to bed regularly at eight o'clock, but as her father almost every evening had visitors, and as these visitors, being Russians, spent the whole evening in talk, it was long before she slept. To lie there and listen to these voices was much more amusing than going to sleep. The most peremptory talk of all, she told me, came from one of the most regular visitors who was a special favourite of hers. Though she did not, of course, know it then, what she was hearing, evening by evening, was his outline of his somewhat chilly New State of the People. He has passed into history under the name of Ilyitch Lenin.

The orthodox Jew is not to-day so obvious a feature as he was, but among the elderly the old customs and ceremonies of the faith are maintained. The Jews are as sentimental a race as the English. At one time the mass of the population were strict in their observances, and recreants were rare; but the younger generation appears to be gently but decidedly breaking away. They marry outside their faith, they eat what they will, they observe Shabos or not, as they fancy; and if they attend the synagogue at all they attend it perfunctorily, once a year, at Yom Kippur. Even that solemn fast they seldom observe for the full twenty-four hours. Still, there remain enough of the orthodox to lend to the streets of Whitechapel Road and Commercial Road East the dark colour of Mosaic legend and the mournful echo of the Wall of Lamentation. Even the insensitive tourist can perceive here the burden of an unexpressed pain. Its older people are living under a weight of unprofitable memories and abiding by traditions which, though they know them to be empty of all spirit, they will not discard. As a race there is no future for them, and their footsteps are a miserere. But they are not, on the surface, aware of this: the burden of pain is emitted by the sleeping blood. It is this racial pain which casual observers from the other side of London mistake for the spirit of the whole East End, and, knowing no better, assume its cause to be social privation. On the surface they are light and free, and they take life as it comes, despite their daily plaint of "Such a life I have!" They give to it a zest and a decoration which are less than Latin but much more than English. The rich material that Israel Zangwill and Samuel Gordon found here may still be found, and the lighter vein of extravagant comedy touched by Arthur Binstead in his *Houndsditch Day by Day* is here for the taking by a new Arthur Binstead, or an English Montague Glass or Bruno Lessing.

They have made the streets of Whitechapel, Spitalfields and Bethnal Green very much their own. They have their special restaurants, about a score of synagogues including the Great Synagogue, four burial-grounds, their own Sunday markets, and their own theatre—the Pavilion, where drama and comedy are given in Yiddish by Jewish actors. The main street of the Ghetto is Brick Lane. (Whitechapel High Street and Road, though largely Jewish in atmosphere, are still a part of London.) It contains everything for the daily needs of the Jew, and there is scarcely a shop, a house or a stall that is not Jewish. There are no sharply defined limits to the Ghetto, but although it covers a large section of the East End and dribbles into sections far from its Brick Lane centre, there is one section where the Jew is never seen. He has never penetrated to Wapping. He is on the edge of it but never in it. In all Wapping, which is scarcely five minutes' walk from Shadwell, I think there is not one Jewish household.  Indeed, it is a local legend that no Jew has ever been known to cross the bridge of Old Gravel Lane and stay on the other side.

The chief religious occasions of their calendar are Rosh Hashonah, or the New Year, which falls usually in the middle of September, and Yom Kippur some eight days later. Then there is Succoth, about ten days after Yom Kippur; Chanukah, about our Christmas-time; Purim, towards the end of January; Pesach, towards the end of March or beginning of April, and Shevuos, seven weeks after Pesach. Of these the most important is Yom Kippur, and the most picturesque are the Feast of Tabernacles (Succoth) and the Feast of Candles (Chanukah). Riding on a bus-top down Commercial Road or Whitechapel Road any evening during Chanukah, one sees flash after flash of unusual interiors. In the upstairs front rooms one sees tables laid for a meal, each table bearing its burden of lighted candles, which are replenished each evening and kept alight throughout the eight days of the feast.

The most important side of these occasions—indeed the most important side of all Jewish religious occasions—has little to do with the synagogue. The important ceremonies are domestic and the home is much more an altar than any part of the synagogue. To an Englishman visiting a synagogue for the first time, the strangest point, among many strange points, is the entire lack of reverence. Judging by their behaviour in the synagogue, he would say that even to the most orthodox and faithful Jew the Jewish religion has no meaning. There is the strange ceremonial; there is the segregation of unhatted women in the balcony; there are the hatted men clad in praying-shawls; there are the Ark and the Scrolls of the Law; there are the Rabbis and the Cantors; there are the up-and-down chanting and wailing in Hebrew; there are the swaying bodies of the worshippers; and with all this there is a running conversation among the worshippers, a casual coming in and going out, a stopping to chat with this one and that one, boys exchanging cigarette cards without remonstrance from the attendants, and officials stepping down from their station by the Ark to shake hands with the latest arrival.

But with a little more knowledge he will understand that the synagogue side of the Jewish faith is formal only; the serious side, as I say, belongs to the home. To the Jew the home means even more than it means to the middle-class Englishman. The creation and maintenance of the home and the family are almost an article of the faith, and it is in those homes where the faith survives that it is seen in full and significant operation. Among the orthodox, meals are attended by many ceremonies. Hands must be washed before and after a meal. There are graces from the host and responses from the company. Even when a meal is taken alone a grace is said. Meat and poultry must be *kosher*, and special knives and plates are used for meat. Most houses possess four sets of table utensils—two for everyday use, and two for use during Passover. The two sets are necessary, because no utensil that has been used for butter may be used for meat, and vice versa. If a knife whose proper office is for meat should by accident touch a plate of butter, both are defiled and must be got out of the house. The most important feature of Passover is the household feast to which everybody, whether of the family or servants, sits down. For this feast all the most precious possessions of the house are set out in display, and all the best cutlery and table decoration is used. The progress of the meal is marked by many prayers and much ritual. During Sabbath the strict Jew must not light a fire or a lamp or a candle, or tend a fire. This law, during the winter months, is a source of profit to many of their neighbours. The Gentile children of this district earn useful pocket money by going from house to house lighting and tending fires for those who may not do so themselves, but are not prepared to shiver through the whole Saturday.

In a strict Jewish household, religious observances are in progress throughout the day. Most of them pertain to the head of the family, but the children also have their part. On coming downstairs in the morning, the good Jewish child, if he be a boy, must first wash his hands, face, and mouth, and then, should he have attained his thirteenth year, must " lay Tephilim " and chant the traditional morning prayers for at least half an hour. This ceremony consists in decorating oneself with small leathern phylacteries. The strings of one are tied round the head, underneath the cap, so that it hangs between the eyes. The strings of the other are bound round the bare arm. A short grace, too, must precede every meal. The girls seem exempt from any practices: it is only the boys who are obliged to go through this ritual. In the case of the boy who is not yet thirteen, he must put on his " tsitsis " or silk vest from whose four corners hang long tassels or fringes, each of which must have eight separate threads. A form of benediction is used before putting this on, and hands must be washed immediately before touching it. In the evening, too, a short prayer is expected from him, consigning his soul to the care of the God who slumbers not nor sleeps.

It is on the English Sunday that one realizes

JEWISH BOOKSHOP IN WENTWORTH STREET

most clearly the great population of this Ghetto. On Saturday mornings Whitechapel Road, Commercial Road and Commercial Street present a scene of semi-desolation, but on Sundays all the local Judea comes out, some of them using the day as an additional holiday and some using it for business. The combination creates the atmosphere of a fair, and Whitechapel Road on a fine Sunday evening is like Blackpool front in August: all the shops open and all the restaurants busy. It is a fashion-parade of youths and girls in smart clothes, and strolling elders not so smart; and Sunday morning in the markets—Wentworth Street, Middlesex Street, Old Montagu Street and Brick Lane—is a repetition of the English Saturday night in Watney Street, Salmon Lane and Bethnal Green Road. This confusion of Holy Days gives a piquant interest to the East End week. It brightens the funereal English Sunday for the English, and it enables the unorthodox young Jew to have a pleasant time on Shabos. They appear to live very happily in these streets. They are no longer true exiles to-day; they have settled and are on the way to becoming English; and most of them are attached to the streets. Indeed, many of the older Jews living in poor-looking houses are so attached to Whitechapel that although they possess small fortunes they see no reason for exchanging these streets, where they have around them so much of the material and atmospheric essence of their own race, for the cleaner and calmer streets of Hampstead, Highbury or St. John's Wood. Wealthier than most of the folk of those agreeable suburbs, they are cheerful and comfortable where they are. It is only at midnight, when all are asleep, that one feels the heavy spirit of Israel and the sombre legend of a wandering and persecuted people without a country and without a king. At all other times they make their particular corner of the East End vivacious and darkly ardent.

Apart from the synagogues, the East End is rich in religious temples. Moving about the streets one sees buildings representative of every kind of established creed and quite a number devoted to what the sergeant called "fancy religions." It seems to be an accepted point among all the religious that if you are going to start a church you should start it among the patient working-class, preferably in that miserable, sin-ridden, god-forsaken East End. Strange that one never hears of a "mission" to the drunkards of the West End or to the corrupt sets of Mayfair. Can it be that the religious are restrained by a sense of delicacy, for which there is no occasion when dealing with the poor; or by a sense of something else?

The gateway to the East End is Gardiner's Corner, where the five roads meet, and its main landmark, which may be seen from many distant points, is the queer tower of Charrington's Brewery in Whitechapel Road. A walk down Whitechapel Road and Mile End Road, and through Burdett Road into Commercial Road East, and so back to Gardiner's Corner, affords rich occupation for eye and for mind. A walk down Fleet Street to-day —which never was Dr. Johnson's idea of pastime;

the remark was invented by George Augustus Sala —has little to give the amateur of humanity or the amateur of spectacle; but this walk throws out so many points that, like Horace's good reading, it can be repeated ten times. Here, more than anywhere else, I think, one receives the authentic tang of London. There is the great road itself with its multitudinous traffic of every sort and shape, its old houses and its new cinemas, its crowding, quietly animated populace, and its varied shops; and there is, at every quarter-mile or so, some piquant side-street to catch your interest. There is Black Lion Yard, a street so narrow, and with so shy an entrance, that you might pass it twenty times and never notice that it was there. But if you enter it you will find that almost every shop is a jeweller's shop. Why so many jewellers have assembled in this alley where only the informed can find them, I do not know. Nor do I know why, right in the middle of the jewellery, you come upon a herd of cows. But you do. In the thick of the electro-plate and the sterling silver stands a *kosher* dairy-farm with a range of cowsheds and a placid club of sanctified cows. These are not the only cows in the East End; in Old Church Road is another byre with a herd of everyday cows for the giving of purely English milk. But in Old Church Road they are not so anomalous as in a little alley of jeweller's shops. Old Church Road still bears the outlines of rusticity. It has a string of old cottages with dormer roofs and wooden shutters to the windows, and an old country beer-house and a forage yard and a timber shed; things which summon cows to the mind. In a street of rose-bowls and wedding-rings and fish-knives they are the last thing one expects. It is like coming upon a kindergarten in Threadneedle Street.

Just beyond Black Lion Yard is the Pavilion Theatre—the "Jewish People's Theatre"—and opposite to the Yard is the very first Salvation Army Shelter, the parent of similar shelters in all parts of London. It was here that William Booth founded that Army which is now represented in almost every country of the world; and in the pavement-gardens of what was once truly Mile End Waste is a bust of Booth recording the fact that there was held the first open-air meeting which led to the formation of the Army. It was opened with concertina and drum, and even William Booth, driving fanatic as he was, could scarcely have guessed what it would be fifty years later, when every city and town and townlet of England was bombarded on Saturday nights and Sundays with the strains (the right word, I think) of his brass bands. But the Army is not to be laughed at. It is one of the few really desirable Missions; one of the few which had a useful aim and message, and understood precisely the best means of conveying its message to its chosen audience and hitting its aim. Laughed at it was, and to some extent still is laughed at, but to-day it can smile at laughter; it has lived through so much. In the past it was not only laughed at; the early followers of William Booth had to suffer, from callow youth of all classes, every kind of insult, jeer, and even physical attack. Mud, stones, garbage, rotten fruit—all these things were flung at them; but neither missiles nor hoots and insults could shake them. Their sincerity wore down the vile pranks of overgrown schoolboys, and eventually the overgrown schoolboys retired in a red-faced shambling, and Booth lived to see himself received by his Sovereign and to see the Salvation Army established in every country and allowed to operate not only without molestation but in an atmosphere of definite respect.

The Shelter itself is not a building of any great age, but it has some venerable companions. In and around this road are survivals of the sixteenth, seventeenth, and eighteenth centuries. There are the graceful Vintners' Almshouses, the greater part of them dating from 1676, and the almshouses of the Trinity Brethren, dating from 1695; both of them proving that benevolence once gave beauty with its benevolence, before Peabody taught it better. There are on Stepney Green, where both Wat Tyler and Jack Cade held the camps of their rebel armies, some Queen Anne mansions any one of which I would prefer to an entire floor of Dorchester House. In side-streets may be seen many an old wooden cottage, and in Great Prescott Street, in the streets of the Tenters, and in Wellclose Square, Prince's Square, and some other squares, are houses that, with a little renovation and embellishment, could match the houses of Bloomsbury Square or Upper Brook Street. If you turn up a side street just before you reach what was once the Paragon Music Hall and is now the Mile End Empire Cinema, and then turn sharp right through a narrow iron gateway, you will come upon a terrace of very pleasant old cottages with long front gardens. In spring and summer these gardens make a picture postcard. Lilac bushes, syringa bushes, clematis, jasmine, and such flowers as the owner chooses to cultivate, bloom there as richly as in the country. Indeed, one of the most profuse gardens I have ever seen, and I should think the smallest garden in London, is to be found in a tiny yard off Old Gravel Lane. It is as pretty a cottage garden as ever you saw in a Birket Foster water-colour or in any one of the sixty-five claimants to the "most beautiful village of England." And it is about equal in floor-space to six telephone boxes. These pleasing gardens and pleasing cottages or mansions are waiting to surprise you at every other turn. Where there is no front garden there are window-boxes, and many a house which has not a window-box has something as agreeable to the eye, and more moving to those who know the common impulses of the human heart. Outside the corner house of many a street, you will see, fixed on the wall, a home-made shrine, bearing a half-dozen or so names. The shrine has a number of small flower-holders affixed to it, and the grown-ups and the children of the little street keep this shrine constantly supplied with flowers. Winter and summer the shrine always has its complement of flowers, if only marigolds or dandelions. The shrine perpetuates the memory of those husbands, fathers and sons of that particular street who were killed in the War.

As you draw near to Bow, the shops taper from good solid shops to little "general" shops, and the houses become thicker and shabbier. Here and there one comes upon a gaunt block of Victorian tenements, and next to it a terrace of old houses that have settled into a social decline. These are not so very old—George the Fourth possibly—but they appear older than they are by contrast with the tenements at their side and the modern jobline villas that confront them. And they give the illusion of long-past times because one remembers that they were the out-of-town homes of those well-to-do City merchants and brokers whose twentieth-century fellows have their out-of-town homes at Maidenhead, Haslemere, Tunbridge Wells, Brighton and Ware.

The most important, and possibly the best-known buildings of this highway are The London Hospital and The People's Palace. The main structure of the London Hospital dates from 1759, but new wings have from time to time been added until now it holds nearly a thousand beds and houses some eight hundred nurses; thus it is the largest of all London's hospitals. It has a special wing for the treatment of Jews, with Jewish kitchens and Jewish cooks. That this hospital is better known all over England than any other hospital is mainly due to the activities of the late Lord Knutsford. Under his chairmanship millions of letters must have been sent out appealing for funds, and they were not the common circular letter. Their tone was witty or downright or humorously threatening or man-to-man. They addressed you personally by your full names, and the writer seemed to know who you were and what your occupation. Each of them was signed by Lord Knutsford (or Sidney Holland before he came into the title), and I think none of them was typewritten. Many of them were written by Lord

Knutsford himself, and those that were not looked as though they had been. His knowledge of what American Schools of Salesmanship call the Psychology of Approach was proved by their effect. They brought in the money when more serious appeals fell dead.

The People's Palace, as is generally known, arose out of a fanciful sketch made by Walter Besant in his novel, *All Sorts and Conditions of Men*. It was in existence, in embryo, long before Besant's book was published, as a lecture hall and study-centre; but on the publication of that book a number of people saw the possibilities of the wide scheme and the grouped activities he had adumbrated. A committee was formed of which Queen Alexandra, then Princess of Wales, was an active member, and in 1886 she laid the foundation-stone of the first of the new buildings. This was opened in the following year by Queen Victoria. Other buildings, a Library, a Technical School, a Winter Garden, Engineering Workshops, Gymnasium, Art School, etc., followed year by year. But at the time of writing most of it is closed, and its future fate uncertain. For this the disastrous fire of 1931 was responsible.

An idea of the vast area and population of the East End is conveyed in the fact that it supports five weekly newspapers devoted to its own affairs, as well as three local Jewish newspapers. They are the *East London Advertiser*, dating from 1865; the *East London Observer*, dating from 1856; the *East End News, the Eastern Post*, and the *Bethnal Green News*. Judging by the newspaper-shops, however, the most important news seems to be news of horses and forecasts of football results. More placards of this nature are exhibited than placards of the regular daily papers. One newspaper-shop exhibits daily seven placards, all of them advertising some unique racing system. Thus :

>FOLLOW
>HARRY HOTT'S SIXPENNY WIRE
>HARRY HOTT
>THE BOOKIE'S WORRY

>THE MONEY'S
>WAITING TO BE PICKED UP
>GET MY
>SMASHING DOUBLE FOR TO-DAY

>WHAT DID I TELL YOU YESTERDAY?
>AGAIN I DID IT—
>100–8
>WERE YOU ON?
>I'VE GOT ANOTHER LIKE IT TO-DAY

There are large sales, too, for papers offering prizes for the correct forecasts of football matches and for those papers which offer £500 a year for life for cross-word solutions and similar competitions.

Contrary to general belief, Communism has few followers here. The people on the whole are like most people of any other part of London and England—of strongly individualist temper. They ask only to be left alone to run their own affairs, and they would rather go short in their own way than be well fed and tended under that documentation and regimentation which are a necessary part of the Communist order. All they want to make their present condition entirely satisfactory is what everybody wants— higher pay in a steady job, and a home to themselves.

You cannot go far along this road and its byways without coming upon some kind of entertainment. There are not only the street bands, common to all parts of London, but odd little entertainments not found elsewhere. You may see the one-man band with which our fathers were familiar—the man dressed with big drum, cymbals, triangle, and pan pipes. The cymbals are worked by a string fixed to the heel; the pipes are strapped to the chin; the triangle is carried in the hand, and the drumstick is strapped to the elbow. There is the Mystic Hindoo, a large plaster figure into whose mouth you place a piece of paper giving the date of your birth. In return for this and one penny you receive your " fortune ". There is the ex-sailor who will let you tie him with four ropes in the most abstruse knots you know, and will free himself in less than a minute. There is the man selling neatly packed " bargain " parcels at three-pence a time, contents undisclosed. This is a popular turn; numbers of people are willing to pay threepence just for the pleasure of unpacking a parcel. There are jugglers and tumblers, turns which, in easier times, would be in music-hall bills. The only entertainment I have never seen here is Punch-and-Judy.

Another feature of the district that might stand out to the stranger is the large number of municipal and private baths. Thousands of houses about here are, of course, without bathrooms, but that does not imply personal uncleanliness Among those who cannot afford the fees of the public baths the tub in the scullery is in regular use; for those who can afford the small fees there are baths of every sort—swimming-baths, shower baths, Turkish Baths, Russian Vapour Baths, Violet Ray Baths, and those which, on the analogy of Dan Leno's egg, must be named Baths. There may be dirt in the streets and in some of the houses, but there is little personal dirt. And as for dirt in the houses I feel that too much importance is attached to this. If dirt really created disease the people of the more wretched districts of London would be constantly ill. But they are not. In many of the back-courts the air is close and limp, yet the people thrive on it; and though they live in surroundings of dirt and garbage they know little illness. Dirt, indeed, has little to do with health or disease. Disease, or freedom from it, rests mainly on low spirits or genial spirits. A cheerful person can live in dirt and stale air, and catch nothing; a melancholy person can live in the bracing air of our East Coast, or in the sunshine of the Riviera, and nourish every germ that is looking for a home. Hygiene, being self-conscious, invites disease and meets it half-way. Dirt and stale air, met with a stout heart that never thinks of illness, carry no danger. In proof of this there is the district of Stink-house Bridge, over Limehouse Cut, which is what its name implies, and which is as healthy as any spot of London. There is, I believe, no more serious illness in the clustering back-streets of this quarter than in Westminster or Chelsea or Richmond or Biarritz or Cannes. (A very large part of the London Hospital's work is concerned with accidents in street and workshop and dock.) Fresh air and sunshine and absence of dirt are overrated as factors of health; the greatest physician of the world, greater than any of these three, is the genial temperament. And the genial temperament is the very currency of East End life.

Burdett Road, just beyond the People's Palace, is a long, straggling road of small shops and small houses, but it is important as the main thoroughfare between Mile End Road and the road to Barking. It ends in a conflux of four roads—itself, Commercial Road East, West India Dock Road and East India Dock Road. East India Dock Road leads to Barking, by way of Blackwall and Canning Town, and thence to Tilbury; West India Dock Road leads to the Isle of Dogs, the West India and Milwall Docks, and Cubitt Town. If you are sensitive to atmospheres and the spirit of place, make the circuit of the Isle of Dogs, preferably at a time when your worries are unbearable. After an hour I think you will be glad to get back to any number of worries if only you can get out of the Isle of Dogs. West India Dock Road is a street of East and West. At one end is the entrance to the

WEST INDIA DOCK ROAD

Docks and at the other the Eastern Hotel. There are lodging-houses for the Chinese, fried-fish shops for the English, ship's chandlers, a Danish café, English public-houses, a police-station, a Chinese restaurant, a railway bridge, little general shops, and the Asiatics' Home.

The Asiatics' Home, or, to give it its full name, The Stranger's Home for Asiatics, is worth a moment's attention. It is to a large extent a charitable organization, and it is one of those that are real blessings. With the Salvation Army and a few others it did and does fill a long-felt want. Before its foundation, the condition of the Asiatic seaman who could speak no English and who came ashore in London was deplorable. He was the prey of every rascal, including himself. He walked not only into traps which had been set for him, but into trouble which he, by his ignorance of the language and of English ways, had arranged for himself. In the thirties and forties of last century it was not uncommon for constables to find in lanes and alleys the bodies of coloured men who had perished from starvation or died of wounds. And regularly they were in the Courts for doing things which they did not know should not be done. The Home was founded in 1854, mainly by the exertions of the Rev. Henry Venn, and its earliest fund was headed by the then Maharajah Duleep Singh. A dinner at the London Tavern, attended by numbers of merchants and ship-owners who traded with the East, brought in some handsome subscriptions, and in 1857 the Home was formally opened. It is a hotel for those who can pay and a refuge for those who cannot pay. It has separate kitchens for each race and each creed, so that every man may have the food to which he is accustomed, prepared in the manner enjoined by his creed. It provides lodgings, recreations, and three meals a day for men from India, Arabia, Africa, China, Straits of Malacca, New Zealand, Polynesia, the islands of the China Sea and of the Indian Ocean.

Here the Asiatic stranger can find somebody who speaks his own tongue, and here he can rest secure from imposition. He can deposit his earnings in a banking account, and he can use the employment bureau for finding his next berth; and if he is without money he is entertained gratuitously until a passage is found for him. In the course of a year the Home entertains some twelve hundred men of various Asiatic races. There is accommodation, at any one time, for one hundred and seventy guests, and the scene in the compound on a fine day, or on the front steps of the Home in the evening, presents a microcosm of the Orient. Every sort of complexion, every sort of Eastern costume, every sort of dignity is to be seen here, all manner of tongues are to be heard, and all manner of secret aspirations and spiritual superstitions to be felt. It is like the Bund of any Eastern port, and it lends a pleasing touch of high colour to the somewhat ashen cheeks of West India Dock Road.

Some time ago there came to me an odd tale which had its beginning here. There was a family in Flan Street who were considerably disturbed by the attentions of a coloured man. It began by the youngest child, a boy of eight, reporting that he had been followed home from Salmon Lane by a black man. Thereafter this man began to haunt Flan Street. He took to standing opposite the house at midday and again through the evenings. He did not molest any of the family or even approach them, nor did he stand outside the house—he stood always on the opposite side. But there he stood at midday and evening, upright, hands hanging loose, eyes fixed on the house. The two girls of the family began to be nervous about going out in the evenings, but when they did go out they noticed (possibly with some chagrin) that he did not even look at them; he continued to stare at the house. The mother was likewise ignored; also the father. But when the boy came out, then his bearing would change, and he would follow him with his eyes. What expression was in those eyes, or what intent was behind those vigils, they could not rightly guess. But that did not prevent their guessing. His manner was shy and furtive, which pointed half-way to some objectionable motive; and he was black—or, anyway, brown. It was clear that he was Up To Something, and that the Something, seeing that it was centred on a small boy, was some Eastern and therefore evil practice. The father, a man of somewhat truculent temper and great strength, having satisfied himself that the man *was* watching their house and *was* centring his attention on the boy, went out one night and threatened him and ordered him to take himself off. Without speaking, the man went quietly away. But at noon next day he was back again; and he was there in the evening. This time the father went out and demanded to know what the game was. The man answered him in slow but correct

English. He said that he had never seen so beautiful a child as the child who lived at that house. When the father asked what business that was of his, he answered: Nothing; but that it was a delight to him simply to look at the child. That answer somewhat disarmed the father; he couldn't prosecute or assault a man simply for looking at his son; but he was not to be fooled. He wanted a reason. He told the man that he was pretty sure a man wouldn't spend hours hanging about outside a house just to *look* at a child. There was something behind it. What was it? The man again said: Nothing. Nothing but a simple desire of a simple person to look at the most beautiful thing he had seen in this world. The father wanted to say *Pah* and *Bah* and Don't Tell *Me*; but something in the man's simple face and attitude stopped him. He reduced himself to saying " Well, I don't like it and I'm not going to have it. There's something nasty about it. And if I have any more of this annoyance I shall put the police on you. See? " To which the man answered: " Very well. If that is your wish. . . . But I think it unkind. I want nothing but to look at him. I am honest. I am not wicked. Before I would do him harm I would kill myself. If any harm threatened him I would give myself to save him." These words, which *sounded* ridiculous, were spoken so gravely and simply that the remnants of the father's truculence trickled out of him. But still he was puzzled and suspicious. These Eastern fellows. . . . you didn't know where you were with them. It was so silly that there *must* be something—something nasty— behind it. And yet, looking at the man, some instinct told him it was all right. He looked so pathetic, so cold, so gentle, so blankly guileless, not with the guilelessness of the child, which is a masked cunning, but with the guilelessness of the born "natural." And one left hook would knock the life out of him. Considering this, the father, a little flattered by the discovery of his son's beauty, which he had never noticed, said: "All right. If you want to look at the boy, come across. But any tricks, mind you, and there won't be much left of *you*." They crossed the road and the father called the boy out. The boy came out, and the father said: "Well, there you are. If you must look at him." The brown man looked down and the boy looked up. The brown man bent himself to the boy's height and smiled. The boy answered the smile. The brown man took two pennies from his pocket and held them out to the boy in his right hand. The boy went to take them, and the hand was empty. The man nodded to his left hand which held the two pennies. The boy went to take them. The left hand was empty. The man said: "Look in your handkerchief." The boy pulled a handkerchief from his pocket and two pennies fell to the pavement. The boy looked up at his father in a sort of dazed delight. The father, fumbling in his Western mind, was still wondering what the game was; but, resting on the strength of his right and left, he said: "D'you know any more of those tricks?" The man said, as though apologizing: "Yes. They are very simple." "H'm. Well, come in and show us some more."

So the man was taken into the house, and the

father, having quieted the staring faces of his wife and the girls with an airy " All right. Don't worry. I know what I'm doing "; invited the guest to show some more tricks. He had the grace to cast the phrase as " show *the boy* some more tricks." In that simple kitchen, in the presence of the boy in his own daily surroundings, the man's face expressed a gentle ecstasy. The women he ignored; he directed his tricks to the boy's attention and looked to the father for approval.

By half-past eight, when the mother insisted on the boy's bed-time, he had become a hero to the boy and an amusing companion to the father. He bewildered the boy and the women with his conjuring, and he was clever enough to treat the father as an equal and explain to him how the tricks were done. When he left, he left not only on the understanding that he might see the boy again, but on a definite invitation to make another visit. After he had gone, and the impact of his immediate presence was removed, they were still suspicious; they still wondered what ulterior object he had in wishing to be with the boy; but their observation of him had calmed many of their fears, and there was still father's strong arms. If the man saw the boy in the house only, everything would be all right; they were still decided that he should have no chance of getting at the boy outside the house. They learned later that he desired no such chance. Having no ulterior object, it was greater delight to him to be with the boy in his own home than merely to see him in the street. The story he had told was true. He was not wicked or evil, nor even sensual. He worshipped this boy's beauty as an artist might, and to this worship he added such a love as a parent sometimes has for a particular child. After many visits his gentleness and simplicity had conquered them all; conquered the natural suspicions of a father who had heard of perverse practices, and conquered even the women, who liked his gentle ways, and set his reserve towards them to the fact that he was an Eastern foreigner and obviously Queer in the Head. The bliss that he experienced in playing with the boy, and talking with him, and being with him, shed itself about that kitchen until the family unconsciously came to look forward to the evenings when Old Ali (he was twenty-four) was expected. On those evenings he was greeted as an old acquaintance, without ceremony; he was one of them. And the first words of the boy and the father would be: "Got any new tricks to show us tonight, Ali?" And Ali always had one.

He was a casual seaman, in and out of London, and on each departure he left a gift for the boy and tobacco or something for the father. On each return he brought exciting gifts for the boy, a small sack of them, and some trifle of silk for the mother. He seemed to be happy only in that house, in the presence of the boy, and after some months he was made free of it. He could come and go as he would; he was so docile and sweet and so grateful for permission to see the boy and talk with him that they forgot all their early misgivings about him. For some time they held an unspoken reservation that he would yet spring some surprise on them, but he never did; and soon even this reservation passed from their minds. He was now allowed to take the boy to the pictures, and to take him to the dock and show him round the boat; to take him anywhere. They trusted the boy with Ali as they would have trusted him with a St. Bernard dog. He was the boy's devoted servant. None of them could understand why, and soon they gave up trying. The boy seemed to them just an ordinary boy, but this queer Ali insisted that he was the most beautiful thing he had ever known, and he behaved towards him as man does behave towards the things he thinks beautiful—with worship and awe and service. On one occasion he came ashore from a passage to find the boy desperately ill. Here was a chance for doing something, and he did it. The mother had been sitting up with the boy at nights, or lying half-awake. Ali compelled her to rest, and sat through the nights with the boy, and during the day, when he was well enough to be amused, he sat with him and amused him with tales and tricks. He would disappear for an hour or so during the afternoon, to sleep, but in the early evening he was back again ready to resume vigil. He did this for eight days, and when the boy was fully well he provided from his savings such a carnival as the house had never seen.

The story has no climax. As casually as Ali had appeared before that house with his burst of devotion, so casually did he disappear. He left, with the usual ceremony of gifts, on a cargo boat going East, and they never saw him again. A parcel, marked from Colombo and addressed to the boy, reached them, but no word from Ali. The parcel held the usual miscellany of Eastern toys and pretty trifles, and it also held Ali's cap—a red cap to which the boy had taken a fancy when Ali first appeared in it. That is the end of the story. But the family remember him more instinctively and keenly than they remember their relatives. All about the front room are snapshots of him and the boy; Ali conjuring and the boy watching, Ali telling tales to the boy, Ali being a bear with the boy on his back, Ali feeding the boy with broth when he was convalescent from his illness. The boy died when he was eleven—knocked down by a car. And so firmly had Ali worked himself into the sceptical family as the boy's worshipper and guardian-angel that whenever they show these snapshots to their friends they always add that if Ali had been in the street at that time it couldn't have happened.

Commercial Road East has not the civic breadth and importance of the other road. It seems to know that it is a junior highway, and its aspects and demeanour make no challenge to your consideration. On a wet day it can be almost as blear and wretched as Cromwell Road. But beneath the merely visual lies more than a common measure of interest, and its neater side-streets offer a pleasant spirit of homeliness and cheerful family life. From these side-streets have come many adventurers; there is scarcely a British ship on the seas that has not carried a Stepney boy.

I was sitting in a home in one of these streets the other day, listening to the stories of its elder son. He has visited all five continents, and has lived in sixteen countries. He has seen France, Holland, Norway, Greece, Italy, Turkey, Egypt, North America, South America, China, Japan, Hawaii, India, Poland, and West Africa. He has traversed every ocean, and has earned his living in ten different towns of Australia. He has been an engine-hand, a stoker, a bush-whacker, a steward, a boundary-rider, a clerk, a deck-hand, a newspaper-boy, a cinema attendant, a farm-hand, and a railway-goods checker. He is now in his twenty-fifth year. And he is representative of many. There are the stickers and there are the plungers. Often they live next door to each other, and play together as children. Sometimes they belong to the same family. One of them lives in one street throughout childhood, youth, married life, fatherhood and dodderage; the other puts seven girdles round the earth before he is out of his teens. In Stepney you will find many examples of each type.

From most points of Commercial Road you have always in view the tower of Limehouse Church, which is within the view also of all ships coming up river. It is a landmark that is known in all seas and all ports. The church itself is worth inspection; it has dignity and personality. It is the work of an architect who belonged to the early years of the eighteenth century and did much work around here—Nicholas Hawksmoor. From him came the three most interesting churches of the district—this one, St. George's-in-the-East, and Christ Church, Spitalfields. They are different, but in the style of each of them he has left, as the artist always must leave, his signature. One can see at a glance that those three churches came from one man.

In Charles Street, just beyond Arbour Square, on the north side of Commercial Road, is the Thames Police Court. Police Courts are sorry things; epitomes of human trouble and human folly. For peace of mind one should keep away from them. If you are one of those half-creatures who only think, you will probably find them comic. If you are a creature who feels, you will find them tragic. But if you want to know how life is lived, and are willing to pay (in disturbance) for your knowledge, then you might visit this court; for this court covers a greater variety of life than any other. Cases from all parts of the East End are heard here, and these cases concern Englishmen, Irishmen, Americans, Australians, Danes, Swedes, Chinese, Malays, Russians, Maltese—in short, nationals of all those countries whose emigrants have settled here or whose ships come to The Pool. Cases against the Chinese for keeping gaming-rooms or for being in possession of drugs are frequent; also charges of drunkenness against those who, in their own countries, are accustomed to take one small measure of thin liquor a day. These are not serious offences, and they seldom carry trouble or sorrow in their result; one can smile at them without compunction. A few cases of this sort remain with me as pure comedy, and I felt easy in perceiving the comedy because the prisoners also perceived it.

A young Dane was in the dock charged with

drunkenness and indecent behaviour. Through the interpreter he casually and cheerfully admitted the indecent behaviour, but vehemently denied the drunkenness. The interpreter hinted to him that admission of drunkenness, in these English courts, might mitigate the offence of indecent behaviour. But he refused to have it. Indecent behaviour—yes, quite. What about it? But drunkenness—no; a thousand times No. Never in his life had he been guilty of drunkenness. They could do what they liked about indecent behaviour, but he had never in his life taken too much to drink and never would; any suggestion that he was drunk was a Lie. A foul LIE. He was a respectable fellow in his home town, and he would never admit *that* blot on his character. Indecent behaviour was different; it might happen to anybody; and anyway he should have been warned about local manners and customs. As the magistrate had no ready answer to this naïve defence, he compromised the affair by fining the lad ten shillings; and the lad went away with a shrug and a grin at the curious *tabus* of these English.

Another case was that of two Maltese comedians. They called themselves seamen, but they were clearly comedians. One was short and tubby, with a mop of black curly hair. The other was long and thin, with flat brown hair. They were bosom friends. They smiled blandly upon the magistrate, the usher and the police. They were in court because they had been found fighting, and one had been on the point of strangling the other.

The one was asked why he was strangling his

friend. With a genial smile at his friend and at the court he said : " Don't know."

" What had you quarrelled about ? "

" No-thing. We ne-ver quarrel. We big friends."

" Then why were you fighting ? "

" Don't know."

" Well, the police say you had both hands round your friend's throat and shouted that you were going to kill him. Is that true ? "

" Don't know. Don't re-member. We big friends. I never kill him." He nudged his friend and they exchanged broad smiles at the absurdity of such a suggestion.

" Well, many people saw you fighting. How did it start ? "

" Don't know."

" When did you get to London ? "

" In morning—yesterday."

" And what did you do when you got ashore ? "

" We meet a friend. I have a glass of beer. He have a glass of beer."

" And then ? "

" Don't know."

" 'M. Well, if I let you go, will you promise not to strangle your friend ? "

" Oo-oo-oo. Sure I promise. We big friends." Whereupon they put arms about each other's shoulders and grinned at each other and at anybody whose eye they could catch.

" When does your boat sail ? "

" Thursday night."

" Very well. You can go away now. But you'd better not take any more English beer between now and Thursday night. If you do you won't sail on that boat. Understand?"

"Ye-e-es. We understand. No beer. No fight. We big friends. Good morning, mister."

"Good morning."

They left the dock, and danced with linked arms to the door. On the way the strangler addressed the public enclosure: "We al-ways big friends. Always. Him and me. Jolly old friends, not half."

Some years ago this Court cherished a notable public character—a poet of the line of Villon, if not of his poetic excellence. This poet, " Spring Onions," was at that time better known to the public than even Mr. John Drinkwater or Mr. Humbert Wolfe are to-day; like Tolstoy he acknowledged no copyright and his lyrics were printed far and wide. He did not make so much money as the more lettered singers, nor was he invited out to Chelsea and Hampstead, but he achieved fame and enjoyed it, and held it with more dignity than some poets of to-day. I had one or two meetings with him, and found him an amusing rascal; more amusing than many of the finer poets I know, but still apt to sink to the level of poets good and bad, and read his stuff aloud. And that behaviour I cannot tolerate even in angels. He was a reformed character, a strict teetotaller, and he was allowed by the staff of Thames Police Court, in whose dock he had in the past made some appearances, to consider himself part of the staff and to run odd messages, to buy food for overnight prisoners who wanted something special, and to do any little job that needed doing. On each anniversary of his reformation he would hand to the magistrate a poem of penitence for the past and approbation of the present, and this poem was handed to the Press box. More than that, he watched all national occasions, and appointed himself Thames Court Laureate; and he followed the job with a zeal that was a shaming example to the laziness of some of our stipendiary Laureates. Nothing passed him. A Royal birthday, a Commander-in-Chief's birthday, an Admiral-of-the-Fleet's birthday, the death of a statesman, the visit of a foreign potentate—all received their ode from " Spring Onions." His zeal had its reward. Not only did the Press display his odes; he was honoured by Royal recognition. It was his habit, when celebrating Royal anniversaries, to submit a copy of the verses to the Royal Personage concerned; and he showed me many gracious letters from high places acknowledging his muse. I have given specimens of his work in one of my earlier books, and I still possess a holograph manuscript of his; for his Complete Works you must go to the files of the evening papers of the nineteen-hundreds. He was a short, stocky, grizzled figure, with a red face and fat hands, and a nose not quite so prominent as Cyrano's. His name was W. G. Waters. He died in 1917, in an infirmary—the last home of many a poet.

A little farther west of Arbour Square is Sidney Street. Sidney Street is a plain everyday street of small houses and a few shops, but it has its place in London's history. It is the scene of the last battle ever fought on London's soil, and the Battle of Sidney Street, under the direction of Mr. Winston Churchill, adds a richly coloured postscript to the Newgate Calendar. The thing seems almost legendary now. It began with the attempted arrest of some burglars in a Houndsditch warehouse. The burglars, caught in the act, shot and killed the three policemen who were rounding them up. During the mêlée, history repeated itself. Within two stone's-throws of Houndsditch, in the yard of the Red Lion Inn at the corner of Leman Street, Dick Turpin and his partner, Tom King, were surrounded by Bow Street men. King was taken and cried to his friend, " Shoot, Dick, or I'm lost." Dick shot, missed the constable, and killed Tom King. The Houndsditch affair bore an identical incident. One of the burglars, Gardstein, was tackled by a policeman. He called to a friend for rescue, and the friend fired at the policeman—and killed Gardstein. The policeman went next, and when all three of the police were down, the remaining men escaped. But by the help of the informer, or nark—a far more effective second than Sherlock Holmes—they were traced to a house in Sidney Street and the house was surrounded. But they barricaded themselves and managed, before the end, to show Chicago, in the early years of this century, how it should do the stuff it was to do in the nineteen-twenties and thirties. They even anticipated the quaint nomenclature of the game. Long before Chicago knew Scar-face Al, Sidney Street knew Peter the Painter. And Peter the Painter was just as elusive, and had as many lives as Scar-face Al. It was a common story in the district that this Peter the Painter, one of the burglars, did not perish

BLACKWALL TUNNEL

in the general holocaust; that he escaped; that he had been seen wandering about the streets of the East End; and that years later he held high office in Soviet Russia. Possibly he did; and possibly he will live for ever, like Parnell, Oscar Wilde, Lord Kitchener, Hector Macdonald, and all those others who have been seen alive long after they were dead. Legends, I repeat, are far more potent than truth. Those of my age will remember something of that painful drama of Christmas 1910, which belonged more to a Central American capital than to London. The men barricaded themselves in the Sidney Street house. The police, armed, besieged them. They refused to surrender. From good cover they fired at the police and the police fired back at the blank face of the house. For two days they resisted the siege. Then the Home Secretary, against this threat of guerilla warfare, ordered out a detachment of the Guards and himself accompanied them. But even with this they were not taken. They looked out from their barricaded cottage. They saw that they were surrounded. They saw that there was no hope of escape. Whereupon they delivered to the police, to the Guards, and to the whole social system of London, one unequivocal gesture. They burned the house over their own heads and died in the furnace.

But the legend I have mentioned says that one of them walked through the fire. This fire disturbed the besiegers by bringing Fire Engines on to the scene, and it is said that during this disturbance he made his escape. It may be so. If a man's world-name is Peter the Painter, one can accept much more of him than one can accept of Mr. Brown or Mr. Jones. Anyway, whatever you think about it makes no difference to what Sidney Street believes about it.

No other street of Commercial Road holds so sensational a story, but they all have something. Some of them I like for their appearance, crooked or neat or self-enclosed. Some for their evocative names. Some for little oddities in the buildings that give a street a character. Some for the way the darkness strikes queer shadows out of them, or the way the sunshine reveals unsuspected features. Some from memories of personal association. There is a little street or tract of houses which often caught my fancy long before I had any personal association with it. It is called Ratcliff Cross Street, and it isn't a Cross and isn't properly a Street. It is, at one end, an empty lane turning at right angles under a vast railway arch and continuing, by another bend, into a row of cottages. It and its name amused me then. To-day I cannot pass it without a recollection of Mrs. Hemans and "The Child's First Grief."

I made acquaintance—I forget how—with a man who lived there, and I used often to visit him. He has no part in the story, so I need not present him. But it was through this George that I witnessed the scene—the tragedy of a young girl. Tragedy is, I think, the right word, if by tragedy one understands a fall from splendour to misery. This was such a fall.

It happened at twilight of a hot summer evening. Neighbours there are neighbourly; on summer evenings they sit outside their front doors and mix easily, though each recognizes a reserve line; and the children run in and out of each other's houses. I had therefore often seen Sylvia, who lived in the house next to my friend's. She was always in and out. She was a bright, golden little thing, as extravagant with electric energy as a colt, and as sensible as middle-age. On this occasion, as the sun was gone and the air was chilly, we were sitting, four or five of us, in the back-room, which George's father had almost finished re-decorating. On return from work he had spent his after-tea hours in putting the last touches to a wainscoting of crimson which went well with the yellow paper. The front door had been left open. In the middle of our low-toned gossip—twilight somehow induces low tones in the voice—one of us turned to the door and said "Oh!" We all turned then, and there, in the doorway, stood what I first took for a vision. Then I saw it was Young Sylvey. George said: "Hullo, Young Sylvey!" and Sylvey, almost breathless, gasped "Hullo!" In that dim passage she did create something of the effect of a vision. Her corn-coloured hair, her bare arms and her bare legs, with the daffodil-green of the frock she was wearing, and her own half-poise of ecstasy, shone through the dusk with a light of their own; she seemed to stand on air. Somebody said: "Well?" Sylvey, half-dancing, said in tones that were half-dancing: "Going away to-morrow. (Gasp.) Going to Clacton. (Gasp.) Ten days. (Gasp.) Just come in t' show you my new frock. Mummy made it. We been saving up for it. (Gasp.) Going to wear it every day at Clacton. (Gasp.) How d'you like it?"

G

George, in the gruff, casual tone he always used to children, said: "Well, *come* in, can't you? Come right *in*. How can we see it out there? Come right in, and let's have a good squint at it."

She obeyed the order, and at a clear sight of her, though I know nothing about the rightness or wrongness of clothes, I felt that her repressed spirit of carnival was justified. By that frock she was perfected. She had always been alive, but the frock made her a living personality; it gave her setting and background; it rounded and presented her. Judged from the rue de la Paix or George Street, it was perhaps not a frock at all. But it was an achievement; it did what it set out to do; and with it Sylvia held us all and made us share the triumph of her posed Entrance.

She came right in and stood in the fireplace-corner against the sideboard. With arms out she made caracoles and pirouettes that we might get the full beauty of the frock. The frock was green with little sprigs of yellow facing; it was built on the model of the frocks of the Italian peasant girl of the sixties, neatly waisted with an accordion bust, and coming out in a full skirt to the knees. I told her that she only needed a tamburina to complete the picture. Compliments were passed on the frock by the mother and grown-up sisters of my friend; extended compliments; with grunts of approval from the men. Sylvia's mother was applauded and Sylvia herself was congratulated. She lived in momentary radiance; the frock was her glass slipper, and her eyes were all joy.

Then, in the middle of her turning and posing with swaying body and arms, George gave a sharp warning: "Look out, Sylvey! Mind-your-arm!" But it was too late. Her arms were out and her hands were well behind her shoulders. My friend's warning did not come till the hands were midway in a return sweep. Her right arm was over a shelf of the sideboard. As it came back it brought with it a half-filled tin of the crimson paint; brought it to her shoulder where it overturned and spent itself in streams and splashes down the green frock.

The next half-hour was thirty minutes of distressing "scene." No agony is so racking as the agony of a young animal, and for half an hour we had to witness that agony. Here was utter downfall. The glory of her year was ruined; no cleaning could ever remove that paint and restore the frock to anything like itself. Nor was there any possibility of a new one. Between shudders of sobs and a burden of "I didn't see it. I didn't see it in the dark," we learned that months of her Saturday earnings at step-cleaning had gone into it, and months of her mother's spare coppers. There had been just enough left for the excursion return-tickets, ten days' lodgings, and two or three carefully calculated small amusements. Not only was she robbed of the glory of the frock, which was horrid enough. By this disaster, she had to face the spending of a seaside sunshine holiday in an old patched, discoloured frock of everyday. Beauty was gone; it had been hers for five minutes, and now it was gone, and she was in a more wretched state than if it had never been. She sat collapsed and sobbing on a little sofa while George's mother and the girls fussed about her with rags and a knife, wiping and scraping, and dabbing the frock with benzine. But it was useless, and she knew it; and her only answer to their ministrations was "It's no good. It's *no* good." The frock was a wreck, and that little room was a pit of misery. Not for many more months could another frock be achieved, and even then it would be useless, at that date, for the repair of ruined holiday happiness. In face of that agony I realized the value and the meaning of money, which I had often treated lightly. I saw then that there are times when it can be angels' wings, balm of Gilead, milk of paradise.

It was a peculiarly disconcerting misadventure, because, trivial as it was in the light of the larger human sorrows, it meant so much. Sylvia, I knew, would remember that evening when she was thirty, when she was forty, and when she was seventy. And the saddest point of the affair was that I could have eased her agony in one minute, and could have repaired the damage well in advance of the time of the excursion-train. The agony revolved entirely on the matter of money; with money, a new frock, as near the damaged one as possible, could be got in Oxford Street well before noon next day, the time of departure. And I could have got it. Yet I was as impotent to ease her agony as Sylvia herself. I sat there like a bound and captive god who could answer the prayer of his appellant if only he could move his hand. But I couldn't move my hand. I sat under a double bondage. One was that I was not known to be any better off than the others, and a disclosure that I was would have entirely altered our relations. The second was that I could find no way of meeting the situation without lying under the odious imputation of Doing Good to somebody who was poor. I was compelled to witness a plight of misery which I could have eased with one stroke, but which, by its nature, could only decently be eased by a near relative. And in this case there were no near relatives with the necessary power. I, who had the power, was an outsider, a stranger, known to this family only as a friend of George's, and not known to Sylvia's mother at all. I, who was supposed to be in similar circumstances, could not make what was in their view a highly expensive gift to people I scarcely knew. I might have ordered a frock in Oxford Street and have had it sent down by messenger, but it was certain that they would guess its origin. Nobody in George's house had more than a spare sixpence at the end of each week; nor any of the people whom Sylvia knew and who might have heard of the disaster. Thirty shillings or two pounds was unknown as a sum. None of them could have helped her. The only person who knew of the disaster and did not live within a door or two of Sylvia was myself, and in the event of the delivery of a new frock, suspicion would fall, by elimination, on me. And then Sylvia and I, who had been casual friends, would be set at a distance. All that was open to me to do was to remove one pain by inflicting another. And I could not bring myself to do that. Even if I had done it I would almost certainly not have been allowed to complete the project. I had been accepted by them as in the same boat; I dare do nothing openly, and in this case there was no hope of making a secret gift. I could only sit and watch the scene, and stifle the uncomfortable knowledge that I could end it.

Since that evening, I never pass Ratcliff Cross Street, or see the word Clacton, without suffering a momentary distaste for life. I wonder where Sylvia is now?

North of Gardiner's Corner is the little packed quarter of Spitalfields, largely Jewish and, within that group, largely Russian-Jewish. Many of its most crowded slums were obliterated when the great fruit market was rebuilt and extended, and its material odour to-day is of fur and fruit; its spiritual odour in the past was of an evil excelling even that of the ill-lit Ratcliff and Shadwell of the past. Dorset Street, now Duval Street, once had the reputation of being the first street to which the police went in the event of an untraced London crime. White Lion Street is also reported as a street in which no policeman ever appeared alone. As for Flower-and-Dean Street, now a street of respectable flat-buildings with little sun-balconies, James Greenwood, who was an honest observer and knew his London, wrote of it in 1872 as the most wretched and most dangerous street in London. No such street can be found in the East End to-day, or in any other part of London. Our law-breakers have learned, like the bourgeois, the value of respectability. They have found it as useful in law-breaking as others find it in the practice of medicine, law-making, or bank-managing.

South of Gardiner's Corner is Leman Street, leading to the London Dock, the river, and the world.

ITS RIVER

ALDGATE, Whitechapel and Commercial Road give little sign that London is a port; but turn down Leman Street or any street leading south of Commercial Road, and you are aware at once of the feel of water and of shipping. You cannot, in Whitechapel, see the river or the masts and the smoke-stacks; you may not even know that a river is there; but once you are in Leman Street your inner sense informs you. You realize that this street is leading you to the end of something and the beginning of something. You note a change of spirit and of air. There is a lightening of the sky; a rallentando of the pace of life. The air comes fresh and cold upon your face, and it carries a smell of ropes and coal and spices and tar. Go a little farther, and your eye informs you. The sea is many miles away, but its reflection is with you. Soon, your eye begins to receive glints of it. You pass a Sailors' Home, sailors' lodging-houses. Men, wearing almost-new suits, stand at corners in that attitude of alert detachment held only by policemen and sailors. You pass a marine store and a School of Nautical Cookery. Through a side-street you see the top of the Tower Bridge and the brown sail of a barge. You pass a public-house dedicated to an admiral, and three concerned

Street in Wapping

with anchors. You see the offices of the Shipping Federation, offices of the Board of Trade. You meet lorries laden with crates of tea and pipes of Oporto. You discover that you are in Dock Street. You see on the hoardings notices of sailings—London to Glasgow, London to Leith (for Edinburgh), London to Hamburg; and a new way to France that few people use—from Wapping to the Quais of Paris, and a new way to Belgium—from Shadwell to Brussels. Over the bridge of the old Blackwall Railway rumbles a train that is keeping an appointment with a ship at West India Dock. Its passengers are clearly ocean-bound. By the time you reach St. George Street, the vague has become the definite. Facing you is the sheer black wall of the London Dock, and in Nightingale Lane four senses, sight, hearing, smell and taste, tell you that you are at the gateway of a port. You can see the water and the funnels; you can smell the tar and the pepper, the cinnamon and the aniseed, the nutmeg and the almond; you can hear the conversation of ship's bells and hooters, and, so heavily is the air weighted with the tar and the spice, your tongue can catch their flavour.

Turn now from Nightingale Lane—which is a genuine lane; it is long and winding and has but one turning—into Wapping High Street. Cross the bridge over Wapping Basin and continue down the street until you come to King Henry's Stairs. Turn down the passage and go out on the Tunnel Pier, and there, on that pier, you will receive the full story of which, since leaving Whitechapel, you have had hints. There the Pool of London is spread out before you. There you will realize that London is a port of many ships. In slow procession they pass before you—Norwegian, Danish, Portuguese, Spanish, German, Japanese, and British—each of them bringing something to the London Dock to feed or furnish the people of southern England. There are John Masefield's dirty British coasters with their cheap tin trays, and equally dirty tramps with their cargo of ivory, apes and peacocks. Among them move ponderously-stately barges and snorting tugs, Thames Police boats and Trinity House boats. On either shore rise the flat fronts of warehouses. They are broken here and there by the bay windows of old taverns. On your right is the Tower Bridge. On your left is the landmark of Limehouse Church. Opposite you is the Rotherhithe water-front, the eccentric chimneys of the South Metropolitan Gas Works, and a dim blue line which is the hills of Kent. Against the sky the giant black fingers of a hundred cranes write their invisible message. And composing all these crude elements into a picture runs the Thames, one of the smallest and slimmest of the world's rivers, and perhaps the most famous of all.

If you are a Londoner, and are seeing this for the first time, as I did at thirteen (never having seen a river), you will, I fancy, experience a moment of such intense emotion that it will remain in your memory for ever. I have seen this view I cannot say how many times, yet each separate occasion seems but a continuance of all the others, and no matter how often I may yet see it, I shall be seeing it in one long once.

There are some moments in our lives which never perish, and it is these moments which *are* our lives. No man lives a life of sixty or seventy years. His life is merely a matter of some exquisite and gleaming minutes which, in a tale of some million minutes, are the essence of that tale. No biography of a man of seventy is a record of his seventy years; it is a record only of a few selected episodes and acts, and these again are selected only from the outward and visible events. Even an intimate autobiography is not the true story of a life; it is only what the author *thinks* is the story of his life. His real life (the intense minutes) is seldom known to his friends, and often it is not known to himself. In a Life and Letters these minutes make no appearance, since they are never the "important" minutes of our lives; almost always they are capricious and insignificant. Yet, in looking back, it is just these trivial minutes which rise unbidden in the mind. We may forget upon what day we were called to the Bar, or elected to Parliament, or met our wives; but to the very end these other, and apparently trivial things, remain with us.

They belong to no one period of our lives. They come in age as in youth—beautiful beads sliding along the string of our dailiness. They carry nothing that perceptibly marks them from other minutes, but since they stay so firmly with us they must be charged with some spiritual value which is in harmony with our own at the moment of their arrival. Most of them are plain matters of fact, without dressing of circumstance or occasion; and it is not until later that we realize that at that time we lived one of the beautiful and truly important minutes of our lives. Reflecting upon the panorama of our life, with its pleasant faces, odd or lovely events, sorrow and happiness, town and country scenes, sounds and odours, reason may tell us that *this* was an important moment in our development, and *that* was an occasion when we were fully happy. But if we leave memory to operate by itself, the things that rise to the surface are not those things, but the little things which, at the time, passed unnoticed. I can clearly recall the thrill that came to me on a fourth (and understanding) hearing of some of the forty-eight fugues and preludes. Yet it is not that occasion which comes to memory when the idea of music is shot into my mind; not that, nor any occasion concerned with great music; but a dim street in a suburb and an organ playing " The Swannee River." I have seen and been moved by fine actors and actresses; yet whenever I think casually of the theatre I do not think of them. I think of a forlorn comic singer in a Portsmouth music hall. I had dropped into the hall to kill forty minutes of waiting for a train. I had no programme, and cannot put his name on record; but his performance will stay with me for ever as the essential unit of everything pertaining to the theatre. Again, I have spent many summer afternoons on country lawns, and, when I wish, I can recall them. But the one that comes to me automatically on the word " summer " is one that I spent on the lawn of a riverside inn. It was marked by no event and no pleasant company. I was alone, and it was just one summer day of many. I have seen more beautiful places, and in finer weather, and have spent many happier afternoons; yet, without reason, that afternoon, by some untraceable alchemy, became the factor of all the summer afternoons of my life. There have been other afternoons; there will be more; but that afternoon, having lived its few hours, remains in my memory as the poet's emotion remains in his poem years after the poet has gone. I have spent many beautiful evenings with friends; yet the evening that remains most clearly with me is a casual evening spent with a stranger in a standardized service-flat. Nothing happened. There was no remarkable talk, no special entertainment; just two unacquainted people, one of whom had wanted to meet the other, sitting together and chatting of this and of that. But some sweet influence must have been at work to bless that evening, for no other is so fragrant in my memory. Perhaps this influence is the secret of these occasions; perhaps these unimportant minutes remain with us because this influence was working then, and was not working at other and more important times. Certainly we only come fully to life when it *is* working. The essence of our being is not in what we have done or said or seen, or what we have consciously felt; but in what we have unconsciously been *made* to feel. And for myself, the streets of the East End, as I have said, and above all this waterside, have given me, suddenly and exquisitely, some of the most poignant moments of this real life; and none more poignant or more imperishable than my first sight, on a dull day, of The Pool.

ALDERMAN'S STEPS, WAPPING

Water is a powerful Mesmer. I could not stand and stare at a landscape, even of the most moving sort, for an hour at a time; but often I have gone out on King Henry's pier, or some other pier, on a summer morning or afternoon of winter, and have found later, when I woke up in Wapping High Street, or the Isle of Dogs, that I had stood on that pier for two hours. I had no awareness of time, but in retrospect I was aware of having known keen moments and of being stocked with impression upon impression. Others know this mesmerism. These piers are never empty. On a warm summer evening, or on the coldest day, you will see half a dozen or so men, young and old, leaning on the railings and staring out at the prospect. They do not talk to each other; by the hour and the hour they lean and stare. Each of them, like listeners at a concert, is enclosed and lost within his special vision of the prospect. It is not a beautiful prospect; in detail it is gaunt and tousled, and if the river were a road nobody would look for five minutes upon it. But the water holds them and bids them to communion, and in that communion they find it beautiful. Like most riverscapes, its tone is mainly elegiac. Under blue sky or wan sky it has the melancholy that is inseparable from water-spaces. A voice calling cheerily across it reaches the ear in tones of sadness; and the voices of vessels—syrens, hooters, whistles and pulleys—all are sad. The wash of water against the staples is sad, the lines of the departing ships are sad, and the flood of the tide is as sad as that simile of sadness, the ebb. But sad as its feeling is by day, by night it is deepened. It becomes then a sort of serene grief, so full, so pure, that happiness seems trite and colour is no longer splendid. If ever I have been near to the soul of beauty, before which man's images of beauty are mere chocolate-boxes, it has been here, at night, under this grievousness of lamplight and river.

There are many points from which one may view it. The points at which I have spent most of my own river hours are the Tunnel Pier, the bridge over the entrance to Regent's Canal Dock, the West India Dock Pier (at the foot of Cuba Street), Dockhead (at the end of Wapping Wall), the river gardens of Shadwell, the back windows of " The Grapes " and " The Town of Ramsgate," and the verandah of " The Prospect of Whitby." Any three of these points may embrace the same features, but each affords a fresh arrangement of them, a new angle, and a fresh shade of personality. By the fall of light or caprice of cloud, the water's face within a few yards is capable of as swift changes as a chameleon. It can be purple. It can be silver. It can be leaden. It can be amber. It can be blue. It can be brown. It can be black. But always it strikes the mind as strange and cold. It has no secret, yet it has the air of keeping one. Thousands of ships have passed up and down it to and from the little North Sea and the greater oceans; yet each departure of a ship from it is as moving as if the first ship of the world were adventuring on the first uncharted voyage. The ground for that feeling of mystery, I think, is this. Look eastward from any of these points, and you look down an illimitable vista of travel. They are the only points of London from which you may look upon all the seas and countries of the world. We are an island, and our roads hold no significance of large travel, no shadow of the world. You may stand in Ostend or Amsterdam or Calais, and, looking eastward, you may see Khamtchatka, Manchuria, Indo-China, and Siam and Malaya on the road before you; but in any English town you see before you only a few hundred miles of one small country. By the river alone can we Londoners look to the palms and the coral and to those nearer beaches where rain comes as drops of sunshine. Hence London's river has a greater significance than the more lordly rivers of Europe, and this significance weighs upon it. Its business is the business of any other river, —the ordered and everyday commerce of ships making ordered and everyday passages to distant places; but the fact that it is London's link with the world gives to it and to the ships that feeling of strangeness which is almost pain. Often, late at night, I have stood on West India Dock Pier and watched a vessel moving down to the sea, and, unaccountably, have been aware of stinging eyes and throat. I have seen ships depart from many harbours, and have been no more moved than by the departure of the ten-fifteen from Liverpool Street for Chelmsford. But an outbound ship from the Pool is a new thing every time it happens.

No modern composer has yet celebrated this side of the river, nor, indeed, any side of it. Other rivers have their barcarolles, and the Danube has its waltz, and the Mississippi its rag-times, and a few rivers have their chanties. The Thames has hardly anything, and, since the eighteenth century, when popular songs celebrated the Jolly Young Watermen, the lower Thames has had nothing. Yet there are still Jolly Young Watermen, who exhibit their prowess each year in the race for Doggett's Coat and Badge; these should appeal to our lighter composers; and for the serious composer there are so many aspects of colour and sound and significance, the ready-made framework for a symphony, that I can only suppose our modern young men have never seen it. If Honegger had been a Londoner we should by now have had a " Pool " Suite or Rhapsody; but the young English composer seems concerned mainly with shedding his cleverness upon re-dressings of Elizabethan airs, and keeping his genius tightly sheltered from the magnificent musical inspiration of modern London. In default of Honegger, perhaps Mr. William Walton will oblige?

The Docks alone deserve a Suite. There is character to each of them. The London Docks, the West India Dock, the East India Dock, the St. Katharine Dock, the Millwall Dock, the Regent's Canal Dock—they have their separate business and their separate note; and collectively they have a poetry which should have made the impact of inspiration upon modern verse and modern music. But it has not. Poets are still tinkering either with the old nightingale and the wind on the heath, or with the new neurasthenia and the wind on the stomach. Yet by these docks they draw their breath. These docks are London's pantry. They give to London the drugs by which the King and his subjects recover from illness. With their

wine they gladden the hearts of stockbrokers, bookmakers, and those few others who can afford wine. By these docks the Christmas puddings of a million homes are made. By their wool warehouses the young men of Jermyn Street and of Duke Street walk like arrayed gods. By their tea warehouses a thousand London tea-shops gratify their afternoon customers, and a million wives are able to gather the latest scandal about their friends from their other friends. By these docks the carman is given his shag, and the clubman is given his Corona; the dentist is given his ivory and the costumier his silk. Not King Solomon or Ghenghiz Khan, nor any of the Pharaohs, could show such a lordly treasure-house as is here contained upon a few acres in a few bald and grimy sheds. Here are wool and corn and clusters to make men cry. Here are gold and silver, and hides and skins; raisins from the South and cinnamon from the East; timber from the North and coffee from the West. Here are vaults stored with the world's sunniest wines. Here is the entire pharmacopœia. Here are figs and jade and amber. Here are attars of rose and other flowers; sweet oils and essences. Here are the syrups of all countries, and the rugs of Shiraz and Kashan, Bokhara and Tebriz. Here, at this grey spot, is the ultimate end of many golden journeys to Samarkand.

If you are weary of the accepted shows of London, spend a morning here, and your vision of London will be widened, and you will see with wonder what hitherto you have taken for granted. The word labour will take a meaning for you, and

THE REAL EAST END

that meaning will have nothing to do with a political class or a social class. You will learn more of the intricacies and ramifications of modern civilization than you will learn from half a dozen text-books. Imports and exports, which have been figures in a Blue Book, will be visible realities.

You will see with your own eyes how every state of the world is bound up with every other state. You will see that there is already in being a United States of the world, and how no one of them can explode or rot without exploding or rotting others. You will realize, too, from the vast inter-association of interests, that no one of them could *want* to explode or rot.

When you have seen the Docks, I suggest that you take a walk along what I may call the river streets. Here is a route: St. George Street, Old Gravel Lane, Wapping High Street, Wapping Wall, Dockhead, Shadwell High Street, Broad Street, Narrow Street, Ropemaker's Fields, Three Colt Street, Emmett Street, Bridge Road. You may not like the walk, but if you take it, I think you will have to confess that it moved you, if only to dislike. Unless you are looking with the eyes of interest, and are acutely responsive to atmospheres, a street lined with warehouses will be dull, and the random flashes of the river which are afforded by the narrow slips between the warehouses will be prosy. It all rests on your own temperamental hues. I have tried the walk on a number of friends, and of fifteen, twelve were petulantly bored and wanted to know where we could find a taxi, and three could not be dragged away from it, even for food. Some, who wished to see certain streets whose names had attracted them, went away in a fret; others found those streets satisfying.

Which is to say that some had short sight and others long sight. Streets can be as perverse and elusive as people. Coloured names are often a false promise, but wipe the coloured name from your mind, and see the street as it is, and you will see something more satisfying than colour. We have all heard of girls whose names are sweet symphonies. We have all heard family-talk of Rosaleens, Claribels, Giuliettas, Dorotheas and Monicas, and have been ready to be half-way in love with them. And then we have met them in person and have been dismayed. Yet the girls are still girls; if they have not the character of their names they have a character of their own and feminine qualities which make them worth knowing. So with these streets. You may have your own picture of, say, Cinnamon Street or Manila Street, of Ropemaker's Fields or Amoy Place, Gracie's Alley or Folly Wall; and the reality, clouded by your own picture, may disappoint you. Manila Street is bare and bald, with no sound or odour of the hot Philippines. Cinnamon Street presents something very different from the blaze and reek of the East Indies.

Cotter's Green and Island Row make no attempt to live up to their names, and Ropemaker's Fields and Amoy Place catch nothing from the magic and aroma of nomenclature. But that is because you are looking for superficial interest, and there is no superficial or " romantic " interest here. It holds the highest of all interest—the interest of life and fact. Look closely enough, and you will, I think, be rewarded. Canton Street and Maize Row may be something else from what you thought they were, but if you will give attention to that something else you will find that it is just as interesting as your preconception. Cradle Court, which leads with exquisite tact out of Love Lane, may not summon up the Songs of Innocence, but it does summon up something of the ugly strength of industry.

For me they hold so many pictures and so many points of living interest and past event, that I have never been able to assemble and crystallize them. They jostle in my mind—Eastern merchandise and the brawny gondoliers of the barges; Emmanuel Swedenborg and Thames Police boats; trips on tugs and Judge Jeffreys; Wapping Old Stairs and the new Shadwell Gardens; Rotherhithe Tunnel and old churches; Limehouse Church and legends of The Old Mahogany Bar; ships from distant seas and the bookmaker's runner from round the corner. And for the eye there are water-colour studies by the score in silver mornings of September and white evenings of April; and a hundred lithographs and pastels in the black nights of November and the dawns of July.

Throughout this walk history is with you,

domestic and commercial London is with you, and the ocean is with you. You will see the gracious old houses of Pierhead. You will see Wapping Old Stairs, where pirates were hanged and where Jeffreys was almost lynched by the crowd. You will see old cottages with dormer windows, and old taverns with red-tiled roofs; some of them having only two tiny rooms. You will see the once notorious "Paddy's Goose." You will see the awful entrance to Rotherhithe Tunnel which, as you peer into it, looks and smells like the descent into the tenth circle of Malebolge. You will see pleasing doorways and fanlights and knockers. You will see one-time public-houses now living as private houses, and one-time private houses turned into shops, and lines of empty crumbling hovels awaiting the order of demolition. You will see several blocks of the Borough Council's fine garden-city buildings. You will smell all the smells of the world. You will pass some charmingly laid-out gardens—the Wapping Recreation Ground, the gardens of St. George's Churchyard —as pretty and restful a flower garden as you will find anywhere in London—and the gardens which were once Shadwell Fish Market and are now a pleasant open space with a wide view of the river. You will pass Swedenborg Street, leading to Prince's Square, where, until a few years ago, stood the Swedish Church, under whose altar rested the remains of Emmanuel Swedenborg. (They were conveyed to Sweden in 1908.) You will meet sailors and dockers and carters and ship-builders and bargees. You will meet captains who have just completed a thirty-thousand-mile voyage, and captains who have never left the river. As you go farther eastward you will meet Malays, Arabs, Chinese, Japanese, Hindoos, negroes; Finns from the Finland Seamen's Home, Dutchmen from the Dutch Sailors' Home, and Greeks who have never seen Greece. You will meet men of most European countries except France, and types of most races, but not, as I have said, in this particular stretch the Jew. And you will be moving all the time under that high grey light which is the light of all watersides.

When you have taken the walk by day you might do it again by night. It will be a new walk, with new aspects, new atmospheres, new shapes and new tones. And when you have done that, the next thing to do, to complete your comprehension of London as a port, is to take boat from Greenwich and travel up-river to Westminster. This is the only effective approach to London, and if it were possible I would like all foreigners who visit us to enter in this manner, as foreigners enter New York. As it is, our railways give them, as a first impression, the dreariest and dirtiest sides of the city; and the approaches by road are no better. We carry them through the slums of Battersea and Kentish Town and Haggerston and Notting Dale and Willesden, and land them in the grime of Waterloo Road or Pentonville or Drummond Street or Fenchurch Street or Praed Street. They do not approach London; they crash into it, or rather, into its dust-bin. But if we could bring them to London Bridge or Westminster by boat, then the city would reveal itself to them slowly, point by point, in accumulating majesty,

THE CIRCUS, ALDGATE

By the Tavern

until at last, by delicate and apprehending progress, they would come, in the right frame of mind, to its centre. From the river it can be seen and felt, in its detail and in its magnitude. Buildings, spires, towers, bridges, are open to the wide view, as they never are on the railway, or even on the road. Instead of rushing through a nest of slums in a closed box, the visitors would come in open air, at a quiet pace, along its main highway, and would be able to perceive, on either side, the gradual thickening of its tributary features up to the ultimate and nicely timed climax. The first trepidation of a great city they would catch at Greenwich—the Park, the Hospital, and that world-point, the Observatory. Then, with reflective intervals, and the feeling of getting " warmer " and " warmer," they would receive Limehouse Church, St. George's-in-the-East, the Tower Bridge, the Tower, the Custom House, London Bridge, St. Saviour's, Bankside, The Monument, the dome of St. Paul's, Old Bailey, The Temple, Bush House, Waterloo Bridge, Somerset House, Savoy Hotel, Big Ben, Victoria Tower, and the Abbey. Not only would they know, as a fact, that they were in London; they would have *realized* London as a city and as a port. Under modern conditions they get no chance to do this, and in the future there will be still less chance. We no longer approach places. We burst into them or drop upon them. To climb into an aeroplane at Le Bourget and climb out of it in Teheran may be convenient, but it is useless to anybody who wants to know Persia. It is like those impulsive friendships which are dissipated in three months. Places, like people and all good things, if they are to give their best, should be come upon slowly. They must be observed from a distance, and must draw us by gradual revelation of this new aspect and that new aspect. We must catch their colour and their vibration, touch by touch. We must know them before they know us, and before we make social contact with them. Only by the slow approach can we do this; by having them before us while they are yet distant; by halting a mile or so from their walls; by absorbing them unawares. To reach a city slowly, on foot or by horse or by river, is the only right way of reaching a city. I wish it were not an out-of-date way.

If you repeat that waterside walk by night you will, I think, be caught by the mystery of the alleys. It was in them, as I have said, that I first suffered the sense of London's awfulness, first really met London; and I have not yet exhausted their power. Wandering lonely and aimlessly about the district, when very young, I would come upon them crouching, as it were, at unexpected corners; and there was something in their shape and the quality of their darkness which charged them with a sort of lupine menace. Each of them held a pool of darkness so intense that this darkness seemed, to my childish imagination, a sentient being. It was so very black that almost it *glowed*. The two posts at their entrance were as great teeth, and beyond the teeth loomed the cavernous darkness of a throat. By day they were alleys, leading from one street to another, or into a court; but at night they were not to be trifled with. They hold this power over most sensitive people, especially the alleys of Ratcliff and Shadwell.

I said earlier that the East End suffers in the popular conception from its past wickedness, and that nothing now remains but the *odour* of wickedness. In the case of the alleys of St. George's, however, the odour is so potent that hypersensitive people should not trespass within its range. There is a shadow upon them and a pressure. I have wandered much at night about the Old Port and the dock quarter of Marseilles, which are supposed to be haunts of all manner of evil and ferocious things, but I have never felt there anything like the shadow and the pressure which bear upon these alleys. The alleys themselves are evocative enough, but it is not from their structure and their darkness that the shadow and pressure evolve. They are charged with story, but it is not from stories of the old Paddy's Goose, or the old Sun Tavern Fields, or the old Tiger Bay, that they gather their threatening complexion. Even those unfamiliar with their story are sensible at night of a something extra to waterside alleys; and well they may be. For in and around these alleys happened one of the most appalling, if not the most appalling, series of murders recorded in the Newgate Calendar; the deeds of the seven-fold murderer or demon, John Williams.

Yet it is not the murders themselves that load the darkness with that extra burden of black. It is not the ghost of John Williams, who was buried at a cross-road of Cable Street. The source of all this overpowering odour is the shadow of Thomas de Quincey's diabolical narrative of those seven murders. Had this story not attracted him, those murders, in course of time, would have been forgotten. By the burning prose that he lavished upon them they never can be forgotten. That narrative has made Ratcliff reek, and has thickened the shadows with a horror deeper even than the natural horror of the actual murders. Into that lengthy postscript to the essay "On Murder Considered as One of the Fine Arts," he put all his power and all his delight, and by doing so he created a masterpiece of the ghastly and immortalized a murderer. Remembering De Quincey in these streets brings the whole thing to life. Many of the points of the occasion are still to be seen, and in the Appendix to my book, *The Ecstasies of Thomas de Quincey*, I dealt fully with the topography of his narrative, and identified the existing places, and was able to add some facts which had slipped De Quincey's memory. The shop in which Marr and his family were murdered, 29 Ratcliff Highway, still stands in St. George Street, but it is not the present 29. It is unoccupied, and its blinded face has the air of having known dreadful things. Seen at night, under the colour of De Quincey's words, it can be more effective upon your skin than any Grand Guignol playlet. In its lines and its form it looks itself like a crouching murderer. The cross-road at Cable Street where John Williams lies is as it was; in the Churchyard of St. George's is the tomb of the Marrs; and the scenes of John Williams' funeral procession, when his body was dragged round Ratcliff on an open cart through the streets where he had lived and murdered, are easily recognized. De Quincey has told the story

ST. KATHERINE'S WAY, WAPPING *Night*

once and for all, and any attempt to re-tell it would be merely to coat silver with lead. If you have not read the story you have missed one of the finest exercises in the macabre. But it is fair to assume that you have read it, and I therefore give you something which most likely you have not read—the contemporary newspaper accounts. These convey little of the inward horror of the thing, but in their very baldness they are effective; interesting, too, as the cold material upon which an artist built a burning tale. And they help to explain why the Opium Eater was moved to write that tale by which he cast upon Ratcliff that feeling of unease which afflicts almost everybody in these alleys at night. Here are the essential extracts:

"*Morning Chronicle*," *December* 9, 1811.

An afflicting murder of four persons was perpetrated in the dwelling-house of Mr. Timothy Marr, silk-mercer, 29 Ratcliff Highway, yesterday morning, between the hours of twelve and one o'clock, by ruffians who unfortunately have not yet been traced. The following particulars are from the depositions taken at Shadwell Police Office, yesterday morning, which contain all the information that has yet transpired respecting the horrid affair.

Margaret Jewell, the servant-girl of Mr. Marr, states that on Saturday evening, about twelve o'clock, she was ordered by her mistress to go out to purchase a few oysters for supper, and to pay the baker's bill. She left her mistress suckling her child, about three months old, in the kitchen, and her master was employed behind the counter, arranging the goods preparatory to closing the shop. She endeavoured to get the oysters, but not succeeding she returned in almost half an hour, and found the shop shut up, and the door fastened.

She rang violently at the bell, without anyone answering. The watchman came up and inquired the cause of her wanting to be admitted, when she answered that she belonged to the family. The watchman assisted in knocking and ringing without any answer being returned. The watchman, who had previously seen Mr. Marr and the servant-lad put up the window-shutters, became surprised, and immediately informed the next neighbour of the circumstance.

Mr. Murray, a pawnbroker, whose family had not retired to rest, deposed that the watchman acquainted him of the silence in Mr. Marr's family, and that he went to his back door, and was induced to get over the yard wall, and enter at the back door of Mr. Marr's house. He was attracted by a light on the landing-place. He took the light, and the first horrid spectacle was the errand-boy, James Biggs, about fourteen years of age, lying on his face, at the farther part of the shop, with his brains knocked out, and part of them actually covering the ceiling, and blood on the wall and counter. Alarmed at the frightful scene, he called for assistance, when the watchman and several others scaled the wall and accompanied his pursuits. Mr. Murray proceeded to the street door, where he discovered Mrs. Marr, lying on the floor dreadfully wounded and lifeless. The party outside then forced the shop door. He then went behind the counter and found Mr. Marr lying on the floor, and bleeding profusely about the head, with no sign of life. He then proceeded to the kitchen, and, petrified with horror, he saw the little babe in the cradle with one of its cheeks entirely knocked in with the violence of a blow, and its throat cut from ear to ear. It is supposed the fright of the mother, at hearing the groans in the shop, led her to leave the infant in the cradle to run upstairs, when her life fell a sacrifice, and the murderers dispatched the child to prevent the innocent cries from alarming the neighbourhood.

The watchman deposed that as he was calling the hour of twelve, he spoke to Mr. Marr as he was shutting up the shop with the assistance of the lad; on his return from the extent of his round he examined the pins, and found one of them loose. He rapped at the door, and heard a voice in the shop, and informed them of the circumstances, when he was answered "all was right," and proceeded on, when he again returned on hearing the servant-girl ring the bell.

The above relation of this melancholy affair is the substance of the whole evidence yet advanced. No soul was living in the house to relate the disaster.

It did not appear that the house had been robbed, as £152 in cash were found in a tin box, besides loose money in Mr. Marr's pockets. It is supposed that the villains who committed these atrocious murders were disturbed by the girl's return before they had time to take away the property. An instrument similar to one used to knock out copper bolts in ships was left in the house, together with a bricklayer's ripping iron. It is supposed that the murderers obtained admission through an adjoining empty house.

This horrible event excited, of course, a great sensation in the neighbourhood, and every endeavour was used to trace out the murderers. Five Portuguese sailors were yesterday taken into custody on suspicion. The Police officers are all on the alert, and we trust the miscreants will be discovered.

"*The Times,*" *December* 21, 1811.

On Thursday night, between the hours of eleven and twelve, another scene of sanguinary atrocity was acted in New Gravel Lane, Ratcliff Highway, equalling in barbarity the murders of Mr. Marr and his family. Three persons, all considerably upwards of fifty years of age, were butchered by some ruffians yet unknown. The following particulars are the substance of what has yet transpired with respect to this fresh instance of ferocity.

Mr. Williamson and his wife kept the King's Arms public-house in New Gravel Lane; and the other inmates of this house consisted of an old woman, who collected pots and waited in the tap-room; a little girl, about fourteen years old, their granddaughter; and a man named John Turner, their lodger. On Thursday night, a little before eleven, Turner came home to his lodgings, and after wishing his landlord and landlady a good-night, went upstairs to bed. Mr. Williamson was then preparing to shut up his house. Turner, almost immediately after he got into bed, fell into a sound sleep, in which he continued for about half an hour, when he was awakened by a noise below stairs. He listened a few moments, and heard the servant-maid crying out "We are all murdered!" Not knowing what was the matter he stole downstairs, undressed, and cautiously looked through the tap-room door which had a glass window in it. The first object that he saw was a man dressed in a drab, shabby, bear-skin coat, stooping over the body of Mrs. Williamson, which was lying at the fireside. He could not see what the man was doing, but he heard the jingling of money, and supposed he was rifling her pockets. His ears were then assailed by the deep sighs of a person in the agonies of death. Terrified beyond description, he ran upstairs to the top of the house, with a view to make his escape. In his fright he could not find the trap-door in the roof; he therefore returned to his own room, threw up the window, and, tying the sheets of his bed together, and fastening them to the bed-posts, he descended safely to the ground, with the assistance of the watchman, who, happening to pass at that instant by the house, received him in his arms.

The neighbourhood was then immediately alarmed. It was yet an early hour, not twelve, and several people soon assembled round the house. The door was knocked at; but no answer being made, the door was broken open with an iron crow. Upon entering the tap-room, the bodies of Mrs. Williamson and the maid, Bridget Harrington, were found besmeared with blood, with their heads towards the fireplace. The head of the latter was almost severed from her body, and the skull itself fractured in the most frightful manner, the brains protruding. Mrs. Williamson had also her throat cut, and her head very much shattered.

Those who entered then went downstairs, and upon entering the cellar they found the body of Mr. Williamson lying lifeless, with a long iron bar under his body. His throat was dreadfully cut on the right side. The wound appeared to have been made in the front of the neck by some stabbing instrument, and afterwards enlarged while the instrument remained in the first incision. His hands appeared to be dreadfully hacked and cut, one of his thumbs being completely severed from the left hand. His right leg received a compound fracture, the bones of it being seen through the stocking. From his general appearance it was evident that he had made a vigorous resistance to the murderers. The iron bar, found under his body, was stained with blood, and it appeared to have been wrenched from a window in the cellar. The watchman, accompanied by the others, then went upstairs to ascertain whether any other person had fallen the victim of the assassins, but they found no one except the granddaughter of Mr. Williamson, who had been in a profound sleep all the time that the murders were committing.

John Turner, the lodger, the little girl, the watchman, George Fox, the person who, with great resolution, first entered the house, were examined before the magistrates at Shadwell Office, but scarcely anything more particular than what we have already written came out in their evidence. Turner described the man he saw leaning over the body of Mrs. Williamson as a tall man, near six feet high, stout and well made. He had a thick stick, with a knob on the end of it, under his arm.

A person of the name of Stroud said that he went into Mr. Williamson's for a pint of beer, a little before eleven o'clock; that before he went in he saw a tall man, in a drab great-coat, lurking about the door, and, while getting his beer, informed Mr. Williamson of the odd appearance of this man being about his door. Mr. Williamson replied that he was told the same for the last two or three hours; but no further notice was taken of the matter. Stroud soon after left the house and went home.

When we before had the melancholy task of relating the particulars of the murder of Mr. Marr and his family, we described the situation of the houses in the neighbourhood of which those murders were committed. The house of Williamson, the deceased, was not two streets distant from that of Mr. Marr; and in the rear of both is a large piece of waste ground, belonging to the London Dock Company, which seems to have been on both occasions peculiarly favourable to the escape of the murderers.

A reward of one hundred guineas had been offered by the overseers of Shadwell Parish.

" *The Times*," *December* 24, 1811.

Several persons were examined yesterday at Shadwell Police Office, charged on suspicion, but no positive proof could be brought home to any of them.

A sea-faring man, named John Williams, underwent a very long and rigid interrogation. The circumstances of suspicion alleged against him were, that he had been frequently seen at the house of Williamson, the publican, and that he had been more particularly seen there about seven o'clock on Thursday evening last; that in the same evening he did not go home to his lodgings until about twelve, when he desired a fellow-lodger, a foreign sailor, to put out his candle; that he was a tall man, and had a lame leg; that he was an Irishman; and that previously to this melancholy transaction, he had little or no money; and that when he was taken into custody he had a good deal of silver.

These suspicious circumstances having been proved against him, the magistrates desired him to give an account of himself. He avowed that he had been at Mr. Williamson's on Thursday evening, and at various other times. He had known Mr. and Mrs. Williamson a considerable time, and was very intimate there. On Thursday evening, while he was talking to Mrs. Williamson, she was very cheerful, and patted him on the cheek when she brought him some liquor. He was considered rather in the light of a friend than a mere customer of the house. When he left their house, he went to a surgeon's, in Shadwell, for the purpose of getting advice for the cure of his leg which had been a considerable number of years disabled in consequence of an old wound. From thence he went to a chirurgeon in the same neighbourhood, in hopes of his getting his cure completed at a less expense than a surgeon's charge. He then went farther west, and met some female acquaintance, and, after visiting several public-houses, he returned to his lodging, and went to bed. The circumstance of his desiring his fellow-lodger to put out his candle, arose in consequence of his finding the man, who was a German, lying in bed with a candle in one hand, with a pipe in his mouth, and a book in the other hand. Seeing him in that situation, and apprehending that the house might be set on fire by his carelessness, he told him to put out his light and not expose the house to the danger of being burnt to the ground. He accounted for the possession of the money found upon him, as the produce of some wearing-apparel he had left as pledge at a pawnbroker's. He never made any mystery of his having been at Mr. Williamson's on Thursday evening, on the contrary, he told his landlady, and several other people, that he had been with poor Mrs. Williamson and her husband a very short time before they were murdered, and remembered how cheerful Mrs. Williamson was.

Under all the circumstances of the case, the prisoner was, however, remanded for further examination.

"*The Times*," *December* 25, 1811.

Mrs. Rice, a laundress, residing in Union Street, Shadwell, stated that she was sister-in-law to Mrs. Vermillon, the prisoner's landlady. She had washed for the prisoner about three years. Last Friday fortnight, she washed a shirt of his, which was very much torn about the neck and breast, and had a good deal of blood upon it, about the neck and the arms; she supposed he had been fighting. On Thursday week he sent another shirt to be washed, which was also very much torn, and marks of blood upon it, which appearances she attributed likewise to fighting. The first shirt she so washed was before the murder of Mr. Marr; but the second was four or five days afterwards. She remembered the prisoner's fighting in her house with a lodger of her's, and that then he had a shirt torn to rags; but that was three weeks back.

Mrs. Vermillon, the prisoner's landlady, stated that she had known him some years. Her husband was a prisoner for some years. Her husband was a prisoner for debt in Newgate. A young German sailor, named John Peterson, from Hamburgh, had left a chest of tools in the summer with her husband, to keep safe for him until he returned from sea. There were two or three malls in that chest three weeks ago, but within that time they had disappeared. The box which contained them was always unlocked, and anybody in the house might have access to it. It was in the same room where the prisoner's belongings were deposited. Most of the malls and other tools belonging to Peterson were marked with the initials J. P. She herself could not speak positively as to any of the tools, nor was she sure she could recognize them if they were produced.

The blood-stained instrument with which the unfortunate Mr. Marr and family were butchered was then produced, at sight of which the witness shrunk back with horror and consternation. It was with great difficulty she could be got to look at it steadily. She was desired to say whether she had not seen that instrument in her husband's house, and whether it was not the same with which her husband sometimes broke up wood? She answered, that she *might* have seen it, but she would not be positive. The question was put to her in various ways, but her answer was always evasive.

. . . The prisoner begged to account for the manner in which the shirt, given to the laundress on Friday night fortnight, became torn and stained with blood. He said he had been dancing with his coat and waistcoat off, at the house where he lodged, about half-past eleven o'clock at night; and his sport being stopped by the watchman, he had retired thus undressed to the Royal Oak, to treat his musician. In the Royal Oak he met with a number of Irish coal-heavers playing cards, and they insisted on his playing with them. He consented, after much entreating, and lost a shilling's worth of liquor. He was thus for retiring peremptorily, when a scuffle ensued between him and one of the party, who seized him by the shirt collar, which he tore, and then struck him a blow on the mouth which cut his lip, and from that wound issued the blood which stained his shirt.

The magistrates told him to confine himself to the

shirt found bloody on Thursday week, to which caution he paid no apparent attention.

Michael Cathperson and John Harison, two Prussian sailors who were fellow-lodgers of the prisoner's, proved that he did not come home until one o'clock on the night of the murder of Mr. Marr and family. The former of these witnesses, on seeing the mall, said it was very like the one he had seen thrown about Mrs. Vermillon's house.

"*The Times*," *December* 27, 1811.

John Frederick Richter . . . was strictly examined with respect to his knowledge of Williams. . . . He remembered Williams had large whiskers three or four days before he was taken up, but when he saw him last, he did not take particular notice of any alteration in his appearance. It did not strike him that there was much alteration in his face. On the night of the murder of Mr. Williamson and family, he heard a knock at the door a little before one o'clock, and was afterwards told it was Williams. He never heard Williams ask his landlady for a loan of sixpence. He did not think Williams was a mariner from his appearance, but he had heard that he was employed on board the *Roxburgh Castle*. He had also heard that the captain of that vessel had observed, that if ever Williams went on shore again, he would surely be hanged. This was an allusion to his bad character on board the ship.

Williams is about 5 feet 9 inches in height, of an insinuating manner and pleasing countenance, and is not lame.

At Inquest. Testimony of Wm. Hassall. . . . The man seen hanging about the King's Arms was dressed in a brown great-coat, lined with silk, a blue undercoat, with yellow buttons, blue and white waistcoat, striped blue pantaloons, brown worsted stockings, and shoes; he is by no means of an athletic make.

"*Morning Chronicle*," December 28, 1811.

Yesterday, the second examination of John Williams, suspected of being the murderer of Marr's and Williamson's families, was expected to take place at eleven o'clock. At half-past nine the proper officer was dispatched to the New Prison in order to bring the prisoner in safe custody.

The magistrates assembled soon after ten.

They were then informed that Williams had committed suicide.

On hearing this information, all business was suspended until the arrival of Robinson, the keeper of the lock-up room attached to their office. Before twelve he returned in a hackney-coach, when he stated to the magistrates that on going to the Governor of the prison with their order for delivering the prisoner into his custody, he proceeded to the New Prison, and on going into Williams's place of confinement, he saw the turnkey, who conducted him to the cell, and to his great surprise, he saw Williams hanging to a rail, which partly extended along the ceiling, and is placed for the accommodation of prisoners to throw their linen, clothes, etc., on. Williams was suspended to the rail, or post, by his white neckerchief tied securely about his neck. On inspecting the body it was supposed that he had not long committed the act; his eyes and his mouth were open, and the state of his body clearly demonstrated that he had struggled very hard. The turnkey of the prison had locked him up the night previously, and did not discover any material depression in his spirits, although he had considerably fallen away since his confinement.

"*Courier*," January 16, 1812.

A most important discovery has been made within these two days, which removes every shadow of doubt respecting the guilt of the late suicide Williams. It was proved before the magistrates of Shadwell Office that three weeks before the murder of Mr. Williamson and his family, Williams had been seen to have a long French knife with an ivory handle. That knife could never be found in Williams's trunk, or amongst any of the clothes he left behind him at the Pear Tree public-house. The subsequent search to find it has been successful. On Tuesday, Harison, one of the lodgers in the Pear Tree public-house, in searching amongst some old clothes, found a blue jacket he immediately recognized as part of Williams's apparel. He proceeded to examine it closely, and upon looking at the inside, he found it quite stiff with coagulated blood, as if a blood-stained hand had been thrust into it. He brought it down to Mrs. Vermillon, who instantly sent for Hope and another of the Shadwell Police Officers, to make further search in the house. Every apartment then underwent the most rigid examination, for an hour and a half, when the officers came at last to a small closet, where they discovered the object of their pursuit. In one corner of the closet there was a heap of dirty stockings and other clothes, which being removed, they observed a bit of wood protruding from a mouse-hole in the wall, which they immediately drew out, and on the same instant they discovered the handle of a clasp-knife, apparently dyed with blood; which upon being brought forth, proved to be the identical French knife seen in Williams's possession before the murders; the handle and the blade of which were smeared all over with blood. This fact completes the chain of strong circumstantial evidence already adduced against the suicide. The bloody jacket also tends to confirm his guilt. It is pretty clear that that part of his apparel must have been stained with the blood of the unfortunate Mrs. Williamson, when the suicide was transferring her money, with his bloody hand, to his pocket.

"*Morning Courier*," January 1, 1812.

BURIAL OF JOHN WILLIAMS

About ten o'clock on Monday night, Mr. Robinson, the High Constable of the Parish of St. George, accompanied by Mr. Machen, one of the constables, Mr. Harrison, the collector, and Mr. Robinson's Deputy, went to the prison at Cold Bath Fields where the body of Williams, being delivered to them, was put into a hackney-coach, in which the Deputy Constable proceeded to the Watch House of St. George, known by the name of the Roundabout at the bottom of Ship Alley. The other three gentlemen followed in another coach, and about twelve o'clock the body was deposited in the black hole where it remained all night.

Yesterday morning, about nine o'clock, the High Constable, with his attendants, arrived at the Watch House with a cart that had been fitted up for the purpose of giving the greatest possible degree of exposure to the face and body of Williams. A stage or platform was formed upon the cart by boards, which extended from one side to the other. They were fastened to the top, and, lapping over each other from the hinder part to the front of the cart, in regular gradation, they formed an inclined plane, on which the body rested, with the head towards the horse, and so much elevated as to be completely exposed to public view. The body was retained in an extended position by a cord which, passing beneath the arms, was fastened underneath the brakes. On the body was a pair of blue cloth pantaloons and a white shirt with the sleeves tucked up to the elbows, but neither coat nor waistcoat. About the neck was the handkerchief with which Williams put an end to his existence. There were stockings, but no shoes, upon his feet. The countenance was fresh and perfectly free from discoloration or livid spots. The hair was rather of a sandy cast, and the whiskers appear to have been remarkably close-shaven. On both the hands were some livid spots.

On the right-hand side of the head was fixed, perpendicularly, the MALL, with which the murder of the Marrs was committed. On the left, also in a perpendicular position, was fixed the *ripping chisel*. Above his head was laid, in a transverse direction, the *iron crow*, and parallel with it, the stake destined to be driven through the body.

About half-past ten, the procession moved from the Watch House in the following order:

Mr. Machen, Constable of Shadwell,
Mr. Harrison, Collector of King's Taxes,
Mr. Lloyd, Baker,
Mr. Strickland, Coal-Merchant,
Mr. Burford, Stationer,
        and
Mr. Gale, Superintendent of Lascars in the East India Company's Service,
    all mounted on grey horses.
The Constables, Head-boroughs and Patrols of the Parish, with Cutlasses,
The Beadle of St. George's, in his Official Dress,
Mr. Robinson, the High Constable of St. George's.
The Cart with the BODY.
A large body of Constables.

An immense cavalcade of the inhabitants of the two parishes closed the procession.

On arriving opposite the house of Mr. Marr, the procession halted for about ten minutes, and then proceeded down Old Gravel Lane, New Market Street, Wapping High Street, and up New Gravel Lane, where the procession again stopped opposite to the King's Arms, the house of the late Mr. Williamson. From thence it proceeded along Ratcliff Highway, and up Cannon Street to the Turnpike Gate, at which four roads meet, viz. the new road into Whitechapel; that into Sun Tavern Fields; that into the back lane to Wellclose Square; and that into Ratcliff Highway.

The hole, about four feet deep, three feet long, and two feet wide, was dug precisely at the crossing of the roads, four or five feet from the Turnpike House.

About half-past twelve o'clock, the body was pushed out of the cart and *crammed* neck and heels into the hole, which, as will have been seen from the dimensions, was purposely so formed as not to admit of the body's being laid at full length. The stake was immediately driven through the body, amid the shouts and vociferous execrations of the multitude, and the hole filled up and well rammed down. The parties forming the procession then dispersed.

The concourse of spectators on this awful occasion was immense. Every window of the streets through which the procession passed was crowded beyond example, but there was not the slightest interruption or tendency to disorder. For the most part a general silence prevailed, as the procession moved, being only interrupted by occasional ejaculatory curses. When the cart stopped at Mr. Marr's, at Mr. Williamson's, and again at the hole, there were universal shouts and expression of execration. A hackney-coachman who had drawn up near the top of Old Gravel Lane, bestowed two or three cuts on the body with his whip as it passed, accompanied by an ejaculation which it is unnecessary to repeat.

From the appearance of the body, Williams is conjectured to have been about thirty years of age. He was near six feet in height, with a strong fierce countenance. When the procession began to move, there were two men in the cart to prevent the body rolling off; but their assistance appearing to be superfluous, they descended, and the body was then left perfectly exposed to the view of every spectator.

The victims were buried in the churchyard of St. George's-in-the-East. The churchyard, as I have said, is now a public garden, and the gravestones which originally filled it have mostly been moved to the walls. But one or two have been left untouched, and among these is the grave of the Marr family, which stands close to the church itself. This is the inscription on the stone :

> Sacred to the Memory
> of
> MR. TIMOTHY MARR, aged 24 years
> CELIA MARR, his wife, aged 24 years
> Their son, TIMOTHY MARR, aged 3 months
>
> All of whom were most inhumanly murdered
> In their dwelling-house
> No. 29 Ratcliff Highway, Dec. 8, 1811.
>
> Stop, wanderer, as you pass by,
> And view the grave wherein doth lie
> A Father, Mother and a Son
> Whose earthly course was shortly run.
> For lo, all in one fatal hour,
> They . . .

The remaining fourteen lines of the doggerel are indecipherable. Out of the grave has grown a lime-tree. Five minutes' walk from it stands the little shop where they met their dreadful end, and ten minutes away, at the junction of Cable Street and Cannon Street Road, lie the trussed remains of their assassin, unmarked and rolled upon night and day by steam lorries and dock vans.

ITS COMMERCE

IN the small territory of the East End are shops as fascinating as any I have found in the dozen cities of Europe that I happen to know. You have not only shops for all the things you may buy in other parts of London, including platinum, genuine pearls and diamonds, furs of sable and seal, exclusive perfumes, and *pâté de foie gras* ; but shops for things that can be bought in few other places, as sheep bells and church bells, areca nut and shark's fins. Here you can buy interesting pastries, and sweets that are never seen in the " better " shops —toffee-apples, humbugs, brandy-snaps, pop-corn, sherbet, colt's-foot, locusts and surprise packets. Without moving out of a particular street you can buy Roumanian beads, pelts, Dutch drops, nautical charts, praying-shawls, costers' barrows, fresh-cut chaff from the hay-market, milk fresh from the cow, flags and bunting and pilots' manuals. There are shops which offer you butts and bends and shoulders and bellies, and hessians and scrims ; and a shop which announces ambiguously but with Latin grace : " Dangerous Structures a Spécialité." There are ships' chandlers and marine stores, and in Houndsditch there is almost every toy that the world's children know. There are shops for all manner of half-forgotten herbs—pennyroyal, saffron, tansy, senna and rue. There is a shop where

you can buy your whitebait wholesale. There are shops for mystic emblems of strange faiths. And there is a shop where you can buy things I have sought vainly in West End shops; namely, all the world's gramophone records. Records of music and songs and stories and lamentations and war-cries made by the peoples of China, Persia, Armenia, Syria, Arabia, Egypt, West Africa, Turkey, Roumania, Russia, Greece, Korea, and the various provinces of India. At the Docks you may buy an "odd lot" of such delightfully mixed matters as lithophone, ochre, Hanchow bags, *petits pois*, tapioca, gum copal, slag, graphite, chicory and spelter; though what you would do with such a lot when you got it home I don't know. Give it to an artist friend, I think, for a study in still-life. There are, in the side-streets off other side-streets, shops which are not shops at all, but merely, as in country villages, cottages which have turned their front-parlours into shops and their parlour-windows into public spectacles and rendezvous for the children. There are shops which, besides being tobacconists' or hairdressers' or tea-shops, also sell hot and cold baths. But most exciting of all are the odds-and-ends shops.

These are not the shops of curio-dealers or rag-and-bone men. They are shops whose stock is new but of such an insanely assorted kind that fifty guesses would not help you to name in a phrase their owners' line of business, unless you compromised on the word Everything. Indeed, at sight of them it seems that anything that cannot be got elsewhere could be got in these shops—if the owner were able to find it. They draw me much more than the well-regulated shop: the inspiration behind them gives such a sharp flavour to insipid trade. After all, why should the lunging spirit of man be dully confined to the single track of grocering or tailoring or ironmongering or house-painting? Why shouldn't the tradesman be free, as some other men are, to be versatile? If Mr. Noel Coward can be an actor, a composer, a playwright, a poet, and a pianist, and if Mr. Winston Churchill can be a painter, a bricklayer, a Home Secretary and a highly paid Sunday journalist, why shouldn't the average man be free to open a shop and be in turns what he wants to be according to the mood of the hour or the demands of the world? They do it here. They go farther. Not content with being as versatile as Mr. Coward, they are simultaneously versatile, like those music-hall artists who, with their bodies twisted into embarrassing contortions, juggle glasses of water with their hands, play " Swannee River " on the piano with their feet, and give us " Annie Laurie " with their throats. You may see shops whose windows are dressed (if one may stretch a word) with all the signs of being, as the schoolboy said of Cæsar's wife, all things to all men. Their owners, in one grand gesture of Selfridgism, but with a lofty scorn of the technical fal-lals of presentation, have flung into their little windows tobacco, newspapers, confectionery, furniture, clothes, gramophone records, wireless apparatus, Eastern amulets, guinea-pigs, outlandish knives, jewellery, Christmas cards, concertinas, tools, toys, umbrellas, cats and fiddles and goats and compasses. It has always been a desire of mine to be present at the annual stocktaking of one of these shops, but it is a desire as yet ungratified. And maybe I am scarcely strong enough to stand it. "Got the concertinas down? Three concertinas? . . . Right . . . Put them out of the way on the guinea-pigs' hutch, or we shall count 'em twice. Now the macintoshes. Four macintoshes. . . . Right. Now the high-tension batteries. . . . Here, don't put the macintoshes on the coco-nut toffee. Put 'em on the baby-carriage. . . . You check up those wedding-rings, George, and Fred can do the hair tonics and weigh up the coke. . . ." They please me and they puzzle me. I cannot see their excuse. In a remote village they would have their place as the one general source of supply, but here, with thousands of specialist shops around them, they are an anomaly—yet they survive.

A clue to the cosmopolitan variety of produce to be bought here is furnished by the names over the shops; names of colour and character. They carry you all over England, and all over Europe and parts of Asia. Here is a random selection: Pomerantz, Frumkin, Yallop, Toporovsky, N. Decent, Wing Moy, Allchild, Eastwind, Longuehaye, Pinkus, Skyline, Spielsinger, Proops, Suliman, Mirza Feroz, Iraboona, Domb, Travell, Sowerbutts, Agombar, Yaker, Suss, Kareem, Sugarbroad, Chestopal, Oldschool, Summercorn, Devo, Petrikoski, Cheek, Fergus, Stockfish, Scampino, Rooney, Yenush, Bonallack, Ox, Sam Shu Lee, Sonabend, Mohammed Ali, O'Finnigan, Booksneer, Chunder Dut, Filipe. A splendid and ready-made cast for that cosmopolitan novel which Somerset Maugham may yet give us. They give to shopping a treble quality. To the common pleasure of the business is added the adventure of the interesting things to be bought and to that is added the smack of buying them from men with such curried names. These names cannot be tossed into the gutter of the memory as one tosses Brown and Johnson and Gordon and Williams. Once they flick your mind they lure you on, as the jack o' lantern lures the wanderer in a dark marsh-land. And you are a voluntary victim. Any normal person would surely prefer that his prescriptions were made up by Mr. Pomerantz than by a vague entity called a Stores, and would rather buy his corrugated iron from Mr. Yallop than from a Corrugated-Iron Department. I know that I would rather buy my cakes operatically from Mr. Spielsinger than have them delivered by a Universal Provider, even if the Universal Provider does maintain the outrageous claim of his title, and deliver provisions to Mars and Mercury, and the Southern Cross, and Alpha of the Plough. Your daily news, bought from Mr. Travell, must surely have a finer edge than when delivered at your door by a local boy; and your sausages bought from Mr. Baconburg, and your new spring suit from Mr. Tweedsome, should mean a good deal more than similar things bought from bloodless Emporia. I don't often buy prints, but if I did I would buy them from Mr. Scornart; his name carries me at once to Sheridan's " Critic," and to one or two friends of mine.

It would be hard to find in any city a more hard-working populace. Hundreds of homes " do something ", extra to their day's work. In Brick

Lane, and its side-streets, all the little cottages are busy with woodwork, some making table-legs, some chair-backs, some bedstead rails, some the beading for imitation Jacobean dressers. (Spitalfields, once the home of silk, is to-day the home of furniture; and it is fitting that the beautiful furniture museum —the Geoffrye Museum in Kingsland Road— should stand at its edge.) In other parts, too, you may find streets concerned with particular trades. Black Lion Yard is The Street of Jewellery. Wentworth Street is The Street of Food. Wapping High Street is The Street of Spices. Connaught Road The Street of Tobacco. One side of Aldgate is The Street of Butchers. Sclater Street is The Street of Birds. Commercial Street (not to be confused with Commercial Road East) is The Street of Fruit. Houndsditch is The Street of Toys. At one time streets were named after the commodity in which their residents traded, or the business they pursued. You find examples of this in the City, in the streets of Cheapside and Eastcheap—Wood Street, Milk Street, Bread Street, Poultry, Pudding Lane, Old Change; and they may be found here in Starch Yard, Cinnamon Street, Milk Yard, Cygnet Street, Maize Row, Mutton Walk, Ropemaker's Fields. None of these is now concerned with its early business, but all are concerned, and vigorously, with some sort of business. Even those streets which have no shops are not restricted to domestic affairs. Plumber's Row is a street of tiny cottages which are scarcely large enough for the ordinary habitation of three people. Yet almost every cottage, in addition to being a home, runs a business of some sort—

tailoring, washing, mangling, shaving, cat's meat, boot-mending, and so on. Literal examples of Home Industries. No labour is too hard or too mean if it will turn an honest penny. In one window is a notice of magnificent challenge: "——, Handyman and General Repairs. We Make What Others Can't or Won't." In another is a handwritten card: "Bring it to Old Joe. He can mend it."  One woman of my acquaintance has supplemented her husband's wages by a most enterprising stroke. She lives near a much-frequented street-market which stands at some distance from the main road. She had observed this, and knowing that things are what they are, she saw in the fact a source of profit. By her enterprise she now reaps some five or six shillings a week, and is able to buy all the children's clothes without worrying her husband. The business to which her observation directed her is announced by a simple card in her front-parlour window—*Ladies' Lavatory One Penny*. A fine spirit here of enterprise and application. You meet it everywhere, but Plumber's Row alone is a sharp repudiation of the thoughtless lies about the working classes and the Dole.

Numbers of the houses of Duckett Street, Ocean Street and White Horse Lane also have their industry—in this case, fish-curing. In the back-yards of these houses salmon, haddock and herring are cured. (I wonder if the guests of the Hôtel Magnifique of Piccadilly ever learn that the smoked salmon or the kipper which they have enjoyed for lunch or breakfast was cured in a tiny back-yard of the East End.) Even the annual holiday, for a large number of people, does not mean a cessation of labour. The fish-curers make it merely a *change* of labour. They take their holiday in the hop-fields of Kent, and instead of returning, as other holiday-makers return, penniless, they return with more than they took. The East End is not only industrial; it is industrious. As for the hobby-industries pursued at home, in back-yard and shed, there is no end to them. Dahlia growing, chrysanthemum growing, vegetable growing (many little back-yards support the family in cabbages, beans, peas, lettuce, radishes, carrots, and sprouts) finch and canary breeding, chickens, rabbits, pigeons, dogs; all these hobbies, together with carpentry, turnery, painting and decorating, are carried on here in yards twenty feet long and in sheds where the carpenter has scarcely room to move his hammer.

In the larger way the main employment industries are breweries, tailoring, tobacco, furniture, ship-repairing, metal-working, feather-mills, leather, textiles, and warehousing. There are also many schools of dress-making and dress-cutting.

One of the most interesting shops, if the word is allowed for such a building, is to be found at the corner of Plumber's Row. This is the oldest bell-foundry in England. It was established in 1570, and is known as Mears & Stainbank's. In this building you may buy bells of every sort—church bells, muffin bells, railway bells, silver hand-bells, table bells, clock chimes, town-criers' bells, cattle bells, sleigh bells and all the bells you have ever heard about. Here were cast the bells of Westminster Abbey and the chimes of Big Ben and the first bells you knew—the bells of the old nursery game, Oranges and Lemons:

> Oranges and lemons,
> Say the bells of St. Clement's.
> Brickbats and tiles,
> Say the bells of St. Giles'.
> Halfpence and farthings,
> Say the bells of St. Martin's.
> Old Father Baldpate,
> Say the slow bells of Aldgate.
> Two sticks and an apple,
> Say the bells of Whitechapel.
> You owe me ten shillings,
> Say the bells of St. Helen's.
> When will you pay me?
> Say the bells of Old Bailey.
> When I grow rich,
> Say the bells of Shoreditch.
> Pray, when will that be?
> Say the bells of old Stepney.
> I'm sure I don't know,
> Say the sweet bells of Bow.

All these were born at Mears & Stainbank's; and Big Ben which booms across Europe through the loud-speaker, and the muffin-man's bell which tinkles through the October twilight, and the bell which sends its drowsy note across the Downs with every movement of the bell-wether—all were born here. Nothing in bells is too large or too small for them. When will a Schiller or Poe arise to celebrate them?

Here and there, among a row of shabby modern shops, one comes upon a shop of true architectural grace. In Artillery Lane is a beautiful late eighteenth-century bow-fronted shop—a grocer's shop —kept clearly with loving care, and almost unaltered from the days when merchants lived over their shops. There is Webb's Wine Shop, in Whitechapel High Street, with a front of 1800, and opposite, along Butcher Row, you have the sixteenth-century front of The Hoop & Grapes, and one or two butchers' shops of the same period. In the little side-streets are many shops with the small-paned fronts of the Regency period, some of them pursuing the business with which they opened; and in Spital Square and White Lion Street are some fine eighteenth-century mansions with beautiful staircases and fireplaces. Most of them are now serving as shops or as offices, and are well kept, but others stand forlorn and untenanted. In the main streets most of the shops have kept pace with the age. There are large stores, such as Wickham's in Mile End Road, and Longuehaye's in Commercial Road East, and all the well-appointed shops that you find in any decent suburb, as well as many more. Commerce generally is taken with a lighter note here than elsewhere. For my part, I have never understood why so commonplace and perfunctory an exercise should be treated with the gravity that our "business men" affect towards it; and I would like to see advertisements in the tone of the following, adopted by our West End houses. At present, Fortnum & Mason alone hold an attitude similar, though on a higher literary plane, to that of these sunny advertisers :

I'LL GUARANTEE to fit you up with a nice home for £15, but you've got to pay cash. Come and see me on the matter. Cot thrown in.
THEN YOU WAKE UP. Nice and comfortable in our feather beds at 25/6. Same as mother had.
ME AND THE TWO BHOYS run this show, that's why you get the goods so cheap.

There are shops where you may buy the works in Yiddish of novelists, and the works in Hebrew of intellectuals, world-famous within their race and unknown outside it; and next door you will find a shop selling tracts and Christian theology, and next door to that a shop exhibiting the current issue of the *Police News* with gory illustrations of the week's crimes, and photographic "art" studies from the latest Folies Bergères revue. In Wentworth Street you will find a pastry shop of Parisian gloss and glitter, perfectly dressed, and next to it the old slapdash Cockney fried-fish shop. In one shop are the pickled cucumbers and mangoes of the Levantines, and in the next the jellied eel and whelk of the city of their adoption. Here you have a seventeenth-century shop, and next to it the glaring concrete of 1930, and next to that a galleried inn-yard, and on its farther side a half-Gothic shop announcing Victoria and Albert. As all races meet and mingle here, so do all styles and fashions.

But, interesting and various as the shops are, the stall-markets are even richer in spirit: they represent commerce in its most primitive and striving form. The earliest traders traded by carrying their goods about and exhibiting them on seashore or roadway, and so do the stalls. In manners and customs they have made little change from their predecessors of Tudor London; indeed, if John Lydgate or Shakespeare were to see the stalls and stall-keepers of Brick Lane and Watney Street, they would perceive little change from their Eastcheap and Cowcross Street. Clothes have changed, but voices are much the same and even certain words, common to stall-keeping through the centuries, persist. Read Act 2 of Jonson's *Bartholomew Fair*, and you will see how closely, in sense, the talk and business of its stall-holders matches the talk and business to be observed in any stall-market of to-day. They sold corn-cures then, as now, with much noise; and they sold popular songs and mousetraps and cheap jewellery; purses, pin-cases and pipes, wooden horses and mechanical singing-birds, as they do to-day. The food, too, is much the same, though that incalculable factor, fashion, has wrought a few changes. Gingerbread is not so popular as it was, and oysters, once a staple food of the poor, are now seen only in the better restaurants at 6*s*. 6*d*. a dozen; while asparagus, which once dressed only the tables of the rich, is now seen on the stalls along with the parsnip and the cauliflower. In more ways than one, the stalls stand for old England. None of the tinned rubbish of the shops is seen upon them. They deal, as they have done for centuries, in the right fruits

BRICK LANE, BEGEL SELLER

of the earth as they come from the earth, without contamination from the chemist and the faker. They are an agreeable survival; one of the few features of old London worth preserving, not because they are old, but because they are useful and honest. They do their business as the great wholesale markets do theirs, in open spaces and free air; and their goods are naked and virgin to the eye, not hidden in sealed packets and soldered tins.

They flourish thickly here. There are the Brick Lane market, the Wentworth Street market (every day but Saturday), the Watney Street market, the Salmon Lane market, the Cambridge Road market, the Coulston Street market, the Middlesex Street (Sunday morning) market, the Hessel Street market, the Sclater Street and Club Row bird and dog market (Sunday morning), the Aldgate (South side) market, the White Horse Street and Durham Row markets, and the Mile End Waste (Saturday) market. Most of them are pure London, but Brick Lane and Wentworth Street are largely Jewish and Russian. There are also the wholesale market of Spitalfields, for fruit and vegetables, and the Whitechapel Hay Market. Until late years this hay market operated in the middle of the road, to the great obstruction of traffic; but it has now been dispersed into several adjacent Yards—Kent and Essex Yard, Bancroft Yard, and Spread Eagle Yard. There is also the derelict Columbia Market, one of the many white elephants which the Baroness Burdett-Coutts was often presenting to London without waiting to find out what London really wanted. Columbia Market is now let out in tenements, and its great open space where the cattle-pens were to stand is a playground.

The Middlesex Street Sunday market is so well known that it need only be named. More interesting, I think, is the Sclater Street Sunday dog and bird market, which is worth seeing as an example of one way of doing business. Where the stall-holders invite you by clutching your arm and feverishly whispering, or bawling fortissimo to the world the quality of their wares, the dog-dealers of Sclater Street do nothing. Their sole advertisement is to stand in the middle of the road with dogs on a leash or puppies in their arms. There they stand at the junction of Sclater Street and Bethnal Green Road, scores of them and hundreds of dogs, and they do not invite your attention by even a glance. They stand and ruminate, looking as disconsolate as their dogs, and if you are wishing to do business it is often necessary to awaken them from their day-dreams by a touch on the arm. Every sort of dog is to be found here, and every sort of dog-dealer, from the man who seriously breeds a particular dog to the man who looks as though he had been stealing dogs wherever he found them as a side-line to bag-snatching. You will see a man holding on one leash a pug, an Alsatian, an Aberdeen terrier, a Chow and a Borzoi; and near to him a man nursing genuine pedigree Airedale pups. You will see dogs of a kind that you have forgotten ever existed. Sclater Street ignores the changes in dog-fashions; it is interested in dogs, and any dog is a dog. If you want a faithful hound, this is the place to visit. There are dogs here who seem to know that their breed is out of fashion, and whose wounded eyes offer you the utmost of devotion if only you will recognize them as still dogs, and give them the dog-heaven of that position which is enjoyed to-day by the Alsatian, the Peke, and the Terrier. Many a dog of Club Row has found a good home, not because the purchaser wanted a dog, but because he couldn't resist those eyes.

Then there are the birds. Along the length of Sclater Street down to Brick Lane are birds of every sort—canaries, finches, budgerigars of every hue, blue-tits, pigeons; live geese, live ducks, live turkeys, live chickens of every strain, and stalls of cardboard boxes packed with baby chicks scarcely the size of a golf-ball. There may at one time have been live swans, since a side-street bears the name of Cygnet Street. The bird-dealers are not so reticent as the dog-dealers. Their manner approximates more to that of the regular stall-holders, and to the squawking of ducks and clacking of chickens and cooing of pigeons and twittering of canaries are added the voices of the auctioneers. Then there are live rabbits, goats and kids, guinea-pigs, kittens, goldfish, white mice, dormice and squirrels; and to flavour the whole there are sarsaparilla stalls, eel stalls, hair-tonic stalls and "novelty" stalls. In this short street there are not only birds and dogs, but everything for the bird and everything for the dog, and a reasonable number of things for man.

Mile End Waste is mainly a second-hand market, a Caledonian Market in miniature. But second-hand is not here to be taken literally; it is part of the jargon of the trade. Second handling is but a juvenile stage in the life of a commodity of these stalls, and examination of their display is an object-lesson in the indestructibility of matter. Fourth-hand and fifth-hand means almost new. Magazines and paper novelettes are still in good form at tenth-hand, and things of more durable construction at fortieth and fiftieth hand. The mattress which you threw out five years ago is still alive, and can still earn its few shillings. The iron bedstead of the servant's bedroom (which was its first home) may be seen here bent with the experience of twenty homes. The typewriting desk which began life when typewriters were first used in offices is here in its weather-beaten old age; and it is still efficient for typewriter-desk purposes. The kitchen table which has witnessed the preparation of a quarter-century's daily meals is waiting here to grow old along with a newly married couple; and the old arm-chair with the stuffing out which might easily be Eliza Cook's, is still, if nourished with stuffing, ready to go on being the old arm-chair to a modern poet.

The Wentworth Street and Brick Lane markets serve the Ghetto. Hessel Street serves the western end of Commercial Road. Watney Street serves Shadwell. Salmon Lane serves Limehouse. Cambridge Road serves Bethnal Green. Coulston Street serves Aldgate. White Horse Street, Market Street and Durham Row serve the inner Stepney. All are amusing places to wander in, whether you go as a buyer or as gazer. There are interesting things to see and things to hear. In Watney Street one morning, when passing down the stalls, I overheard a scrap of talk between two stall-holders.

Both were loudly crying their wares, but between bawls one turned to the other and spoke *sotto voce*: "*Weigh 'em up, weigh 'em up, weigh 'em up, here's yer lovely 'marters.* . . . Yes, perhaps so, but to my mind the two loveliest things God's given us is a garden when the roses are out and a good church organ. . . . *Weigh 'em up, weigh 'em up, weigh 'em up.*" One interesting point thrown up by a study of them is the Londoner's love of feeding on his feet, as though life were a continual Passover and he were awaiting the word "Go!" In many occupations, of course, it is. Taxi-drivers, scavengers, draymen, watchmen, policemen, watermen, and general errand-runners can get but one good meal during the day, and they must snatch a bite here and there as opportunity offers, and must always be within earshot and eyeshot of their duties. Hence the popularity of those stalls which offer food for immediate eating—the ice-cream stall, the whelk stall, the jellied-eel stall, the sausage-roll stall, the saveloy stall, and the Hot Dog and apple-fritter stall from America. They were invented to meet the exigen-

cies of the truly hard-workers. Here gather the day-toilers to take, with one ear cocked for the alarum, their lunch or brunch and their dinner or teaner, as, at a later hour, the night-toilers gather about the coffee-stall to take their supper or brupper.

But there are others whose occasions do not demand the hasty snack but who yet love to feed standing up. And I sympathize with them. I could not stand up, as some do, to the counter of a shop, or even sit at the counter of a shop, as men do at Pimm's and Henry's and White's oyster bars. But at the open-air stall—or, as the learned stall-holders have it, the *al fresco* caravanserai—one's instinct is to stand. Air and space demand the virile attitude where the dining-room demands the social and relaxed. The hard-boiled egg, the saveloy, the whelk and the jellied eel are only rightly taken when taken under the sky and on one's feet. Table and cloth and chair for them are æsthetically wrong. A snack is a snack, and its original sense of portion requires that it should not be treated as a whole—that is, as a meal. It should be taken in business style as a hurried pause in a journey, and salted by gossip with the Bartholomew Fair throwback who keeps the stall.

The Londoner has many physical qualities that mark him from the countryman, but I think the quality that most marks him is the strength of his legs and feet. He seems only to be comfortable on his feet, and the fact that he will take his food on his feet when he could sit shows his great foot-strength. The countryman—even the young countryman—sits down whenever he can. The northern workman does not lounge at street corners; he squats against walls. He sits down to his drink and his smoke and his food, and, where possible, sits down to work. But the Cockney goes to his work on his feet, standing in tubes, trains, and trams; he will stand up at his desk when he might sit; he will stand up to his drink when chairs and tables are available; he will stand on railway platforms; he will stand for hours on the edge of the pavement without even the support of a lamp-post, and he even carries his restlessness into his own home. There is the fireside, and there are the old arm-chair and the slippers, but in practice he spends more time standing up, with his back to the fire, than in the old arm-chair. Perhaps it is this love of the erect posture that has made us the commanding people that we are. I don't know. But any true painting of a typical Londoner would have to present him on his feet; for that is his most self-expressive posture. He is by nature a foot-slogger, and in the humbler world he adds to his other foot activities the business of eating on his feet. And he enjoys these stand-up snacks. The jellied-eel stall and the whelk stall are always busy. Wherever you see them about this district you seldom see them disengaged. Men who are in no way pressed for time will take their midday meal or their elevenses in this fashion, and if these stalls were to provide chairs for their customers I warrant that none of them would be used. Men would still prefer to stand and stare and chew, like one of W. H. Davies' admirable cows.

To see the stall-markets at their best you should see them at Christmas-time. Christmas, that High

Mass of the English shop-keeper's religion, may be fading into a spiritless formality, but here it still lives, if not in spiritual fullness at least in physical activity. Nobody can restore the spirit to an occasion, once it has fled, but its pulses can be galvanized, and they are. At this season the stalls express the high fruitfulness of our English fields and the quiet cheerfulness of the English heart. Some hasty observers see in these massive assemblies of food a sign of an orgy, of selfish gluttony. They are wrong. All this concern with plenteous food is expressive of hospitality; it is not the gross Englishman's dream of gorging himself, but his dream of entertaining his friends. Wandering through these markets in the afternoon twilights of Christmas week one may come very close to the pagan significance of the feast of Christmas. Christmas bawls at you, sings at you, flashes at you, and whirls all about you. Every Saturday night the stall-markets live in the spirit of carnival, but Christmas week is a hundred Saturday nights in one. For Christmas is the one yearly chance given to the poor of having and sharing with their friends what the patrons of the best hotels may have every night of the week; and they make the most of it. So they should. If you are going to have a carnival, have it, and have it with every proper circumstance of free movement, free voice, and folly. Make your streets bazaars and your stalls transformation-scenes. Live for a day or two in pantomime. That is how the stalls do it, and I wish all our streets would do it. The flare and display and noise and cheerful back-chat can almost make one believe that Christmas is still a feast and not a mere function. When, through the damp dusk and against the indigo streets, the stalls shoot their vistas of high colour and send up a gold mist as of incense to the god of feasting; when all the crowd is centred on holiday and fireside, and the jostling of other people makes for grateful warmth rather than irritation; then, in their nocturnal opulence and glitter, they are the Western balance of the Eastern bazaars of Bethlehem and Jerusalem under the blaze and blue of Eastern mornings.

Officially, of course, the Ghetto has no concern with Christmas, and its shops and stalls pursue their business on Christmas Day and Boxing Day, as on other days. But it does not disdain to profit by the Christian feast, and the Wentworth Street stalls are as busy with Christmas matters as the others. Often it happens that the Jewish Feast of Maccabeus falls very close to the English Christmas, and then two feasts, of widely different ceremonies, may be observed almost side by side and in the same streets. While one family is decorating a Christmas tree with gauds and baubles from the stalls, and wrapping up " useful presents " and stirring the pudding and stuffing the turkey, and hanging up stockings, the next-door family is kindling with childish glee the eight Chanukah candles, and joyously bursting into the old hymnal refrain of " Moöz Tsür " to celebrate their deliverance from tyrant hands.

All sorts of Christmases are kept in the East End. There is Christmas in the English Sailors' Homes, complete with puddings, mince-pies, and crackers. There is Christmas in the Salvation

Army Hostels, with a more than usual stressing of its religious aspect. There is the Scandinavian Christmas in the Danish and Norwegian Sailors' Homes—very pretty. And there is the Christmas in the Asiatics' Home in West India Dock Road —a Christmas observed for those Malays, Hindoos, Burmese, Cingalese, Africans, Arabs, and Persians who have been converted to Christianity. The services are conducted in seven or eight languages, according to the races represented in the company, and after the service there is the usual Christmas. Then you may see a version of " Christmas Day in the Workhouse " played to a company of black, gold, brown, and olive faces, some turbaned, some ringleted, some with ear-rings, some with fuzzy hair, some with beards, and all effusing goodwill toward men. There is the Russian Christmas of Spitalfields with its own simple and pleasing ceremonies and customs and foods; and there is the Christmas of the half-Chinese in Limehouse.

For the full Chinese the important ceremony of their year is the New Year, which falls variously at the end of January or the beginning of February; but there are in Limehouse a number of Chinese who have lost the faith of their fathers, and a number who have married white girls and have no objection to sharing an extra feast, even if it is none of theirs. Where there are children of these mixed marriages, it is kept as in any other English home, and little John Henry Kwang of Pennyfields will hang up his stocking with the children of Brixton and Camden Town. And will no doubt find in it much more exciting things than they will find in theirs. If his father keeps a store, then

Christmas will be a carnival of colour, for in these stores is much material for festivity that other households could not buy. There are banners of red and gold, fearful masks of scarlet and blue, paper mottoes, gaudy ginger jars, brilliant paper flowers, embroidered silks, gay brocades, lanterns in the form of dragons, birds, snakes and butterflies. Though the meal may not conform to English custom in its dishes, it will conform in the matter of quantity, for Chinese hospitality makes North Country hospitality look stinted. Elsewhere in the quarter they go about their business as an English colony in the East goes about its business in the midst of native feasts. Most of the shops remain open, and though little business is done, since the English customers are otherwise engaged, the day passes as other days, and ends with dice or puckapoo. The local branch of the Salvation Army—which numbers some Chinese converts—usually holds an open-air meeting near the Causeway, with carols and prayers; and other street missions do their best to emphasize the fact of Christmas to the Causeway and Pennyfields. But the quarter remains impassive, looking on with blank eyes at the quaint antics and barbaric customs of the West. When they celebrate a feast they do it with grace and light and art; even their funerals are pageants of white; and to them the thickness and heaviness of our Western ceremonies of rejoicing must be one more proof of the barbaric origins of the new world.

Food and clothes, as I have said, are the principal concern of the East End, and while I cannot speak of its clothes, I can say that there is very good feeding to be had here. As good, indeed, though not as tricked out and garnished, as in the West. The service is rough and ready, and the dishes are plain, but in a notable number of places the materials are good and the cooking is good. The only thing about them that is really low is the price. Lower still is the price of the Good Pull Ups for Carmen. Many of these, though very rough in service, can give you an excellent plain meal. Of course, the restaurants here, as elsewhere, are various in quality, and it takes time, and much trial and error, to sort the good from the bad; but when you do find a good place you find something which will tempt you away from Soho. Their chief interest for me is that they serve dishes which are no longer served on the other side of the Pump. You can get here an old Suffolk delicacy which I knew as a child, and have never been able to buy elsewhere—pudding-pie. You can get bacon-pudding, a good dish, made in the manner of Swiss Roll. You can get faggots and pease-pudding. You can get broccoli and turnip-tops, which are as piquant green vegetables as spinach, and far above cabbage. You can get very good bread-pudding which, when it is good, is as good as anything need be. You can get stewed eels and eel-pie, cow-heel and pig's trotters and sheep's trotters and sheep's tongues; delicate dishes which would be in high favour in the West End if they weren't a favourite food of working people. And you can get lamb's fry; and why anybody should return from France and talk with an air of epicurism of that stinking mess of left-over odds of fish called bouillabaisse (originally a dish of the

French poor) when he would recoil in English-gentleman snobbery from any suspicion of dining on those excellent dishes of the English poor, lamb's fry and cow-heel, I don't know. The ways of the sahib are hidden in the quabbalah. I have had meals here of every sort; meals in the Good Pull Ups, meals in *kosher* restaurants, meals on barges, meals on liners in dock (I remember a dish of curried fruit which crowned a meal on a Commonwealth Liner) meals in a dock canteen, meals in Chinese restaurants, meals in fried-fish shops, meals in the street; Danish meals, East African meals, public-house meals, and many a domestic meal with families of every condition. Most of them were plainly good; a few were memorable in their goodness, and some memorable in their badness.

At the smaller Good Pull Ups there is seldom a written bill of fare. Usually the waitress recites to you the day's doings.

" What's on to-day ? "

" Let—me—see—there's . . ." This is used as a recitative before the aria. " Let—me—see—there's——" and then in a running monotone: " mun-broth baked sheepsart liveranbacon iristoo coweeel ros-beef-yorkshire. And—Then—There's —gol'nroll'n apple pie'n baked-jam. Iristoo's good to-day. . . . Right." Your order passes below: " Stoo, tops—one." Sometimes these restaurants are styled " The Little Wonder " or " The Goodfare " or " The Carlton," but more usually their style is " Fred's " or " Joe's " or " Happy Jack's " or " Ole Bill's "—after a custom centuries old in all countries and all ranks. The London ordinaries of the seventeenth century were styled in that fashion—" Pontack's," " Locket's," " Ned's," " Beaujeu's." The coffee-houses of the eighteenth century were similarly styled—" Tom's," " Will's," " Groom's," " Jonathan's," " Giles'." The chop-houses of the nineteenth century were " William's," " Thomas's," " Robert's," " Dolly's," and the custom survives to-day, not only in the Good Pull Ups but in " Simpson's," " Rule's," " Sweeting's," " Scott's," " Snow's," " Romano's," and " Driver's."

Next to the Good Pull Ups, the most numerous restaurants are the *kosher* restaurants of the Ghetto; and those whose taste is for rich foods have ample opportunities for unslimming. In a purely personal preference I mention Silberstein's, Abrahamson's, Goide's and The Nag's Head. A typical Jewish dinner would be—chopped chicken liver with pounded egg, pickled cucumber and chreyn (horse-radish) as *hors d'œuvres*; some gefilte fish; lokshen soup (soup comes after fish); roast chicken and vegetables; and schtrudel—a pastry roll of jam and raisins and candied peel. With the meal is served a variety of breads—egg cholla, begels and pretzels (flavoured with caraway seed and poppy seed) but, of course, no butter. Their wines are a trifle too sweet to English taste; lager is the better drink; and Russian tea makes a better conclusion than coffee.

One marked trait of this district is the agreeable manners one encounters. In the streets, the restaurants, or other public places, people do not stare at you as they do in other quarters. However odd your appearance may be, or however

JEWISH RESTAURANT IN BRICK LANE

peculiar your behaviour, nobody will embarrass you by looks or comments. On entering a restaurant you do not meet the hard glares that you meet on entering places of more dignified pretensions. You may be what you like and do what you like, and nobody will worry you. At a certain restaurant in Mile End Road I sat near a comfortable mother and her grown-up son. The mother appeared to be endeavouring to comfort her son upon some shock or trouble he was under. His face was drawn, and he appeared to be on the verge of breakdown. At the end of the meal the mother left first. On parting, she stood over her son; then put both arms round his shoulders, kissed him, and said: " Well, brace up, son. These things happen. You got to face it. It's hard, but you'll come through all right. Good-bye, my darling." The son got up, embraced his mother in his turn, kissed her four times, said " I'll try, darling," and sat down and covered his face. The restaurant was thick with people, and not a single person took the smallest apparent notice of that incident.

In the Chinese streets of Limehouse—the Causeway, Pennyfields, West India Dock Road—are some native restaurants. At one time they were numerous, but to-day there are more Chinese restaurants in Soho than in the quarter itself. They are sufficient, however, to the needs of the colony, and they are perhaps more interesting than those of Soho, since they do not concern themselves with appointments or display for the beguiling of the barbarians; there is nothing flamingly Oriental about them. They are just

THE REAL EAST END

eating-houses, serving the usual dishes of southern China. The basis of Chinese cooking is stewing and frying, and their chief materials are chicken, pork and duck; flour-pastes from lily-root flour, water-chestnuts, bamboo shoots, sesamum seeds, bean-cake, dried mushrooms, dried seaweed and rice. The usual dishes are noodles, moist or dry, of pork or chicken, with mushrooms or bamboo shoots; chop sueys of pork and bean sprout; rice dishes, with prawns, eggs and pork; pickled eggs; and various interesting fruits—ginger, li-chee, longan, cumquicks, lotus seeds, honey dates. A piquant side-dish is their sweet onions. With the meal one takes right China teas, which may be selected from five or six different growths, whose very names are a perfumed garden, as Loong Chen, Suey Sen, O Loog, Shou Mee, Sin Chon, and Luk On.

Down by the river are one or two Scandinavian eating-houses, and in St. George's is The Ethiopan Café—interesting if you are prepared to find interest. France, I believe, has but one representative, The Bonbonnière, though there is "Jock's Lodge" which, after threatening through its name haggis and cockaleekie, lifts the threat with the legend *Ici on parle français*. And there is a café for Roumanian dishes at Little Turner Street, Commercial Road. For good plain English food I recommend the good public-house, but I must leave you to make your own discoveries. The best food, here as in other parts of the world, is to be had at the small, unassuming, intimate places. I don't mean that all small, unassuming, intimate places are good, but it is among such places that you will find the good ones.

The East End has a number of interesting taverns, and some of the most fanciful signs are to be found here. To make a random selection, there are The China Ship, The Baker & Basket, The New York Stores, The Blind Beggar, The Prospect of Whitby, The Town of Ramsgate, The Grave Maurice, The Mariner's Arms, The Star of the East, Mrs. Grundy's Arms, The London Hospital (alluring sign for a house of entertainment), The Havering Bower, The Salmon & Ball, The Horse & Leaping-Bar, The Bird in Hand, The Bombay Grab, The Horn of Plenty, The Hayfield, The Old Friends, The Golden Heart, The Colleen Bawn, The Brewer's Hall, The Blade Bone, The Magnet & Dewdrop, The Still & Star, The Bell & Mackerel, The Refiner's Arms, The Darby & Joan, The Coal-meter's Arms and The Ben Jonson. The last is a pleasant touch. How few of our toping poets are thus celebrated. For that matter, how few of our great are in any way celebrated in London. Our taverns offer a great opportunity for repairing this omission. If we cannot, in the Latin manner, honour our great men by fixing their fame in the names of our highways, we could consecrate them in a tavern-sign. We have already far too many Red Lions and White Horses and Brown Bears; a Boswell's Head, a

Charles Lamb's Head, a Beaumont's Head, a Morland's Head, a Pepys' Head, a Wren's Head, would be a welcome change and would lend a pleasant touch to the atmosphere of the particular house. There is, in the City, the Dr. Butler's Head, and, in North London, the Sir Richard Steele; but those, and this Ben Jonson and The Dean Swift (also in Stepney) are all that I know of taverns celebrant of tavern men.

The East End has to-day but a third of the taverns it once had. Many of the defunct can still be identified, and some—Paddy's Goose in St. George Street, The Old Mahogany Bar in Gracie's Alley, and The Edinburgh Castle in Limehouse—are still as they were, though working now in the odour of sanctity as coffee-rooms and recreation centres. In the whole of that long street which is named, at intervals, St. George Street, Shadwell High Street, Broad Street and Medland Street, once a street of taverns, there are now but six or seven; with the natural result, which anybody but your intemperate temperance reformer would have foreseen, that these few are often overcrowded.

The most pleasing to the eye, I think, is The Hoop & Grapes, at Aldgate—a late seventeenth-century house. It has a massive oak door, small-paned windows, some panelling, a finely proportioned staircase, a gabled front and back, and handsomely carved doorposts. In its early history it was the home and business place of a prosperous vintner, a trade to which Aldgate, by its neighbourhood to the docks, was peculiarly suited. Two establishments, dating from the early days, survive in Webb's Old Wine Shop and the premises of Messrs. Coates; and in Jewry Street is Messrs. Koenen's Hock and Moselle House. Vine Street, off the Minories, perpetuates the association.

The riverside taverns—The China Ship, The Turk's Head, The Town of Ramsgate, The Prospect of Whitby, The Grapes—have something of the air of village inns. They are old, with small rooms, low ceilings, and that feeling of snugness and ease which is given to a tavern only after it has had long and intimate association with men. In many of them the advertised drink is " Coffee and Rum." The China Ship overlooks Wapping Basin, The Town of Ramsgate stands alongside Wapping Old Stairs, The Prospect of Whitby is in Wapping Wall, and The Grapes overlooks Limehouse Reach. These taverns have the air of being big with story, but it is not easy to come at one. Legends gather thickly about every old inn, but facts, as I have said earlier, have a way of dropping off and dying. There is material to supply half a dozen Scheherazades in the *legends* of our inns, but for the historian there is scarcely enough for a brief essay. Nothing is provably known of these river taverns; even the basis of their names is unknown. Not, perhaps, that it matters: the names are sufficient in themselves, since they provide play for fancy. All of them are typical taverns belonging to a time when the word " Tavern " had its meaning. As late as the early nineteenth century Wapping High Street and Wapping Wall alone held thirty-six alehouses; those that we now have are the defiant Old Guard and still full of life.

A house whose sign puzzled me for some time is The Coal-meter's Arms. This is a little village inn, with front and back entrances, locked inside London. You get to it up a passage leading off Old Church Road. I could not think what a coal-meter was. I had heard of gas-meters and water-meters, but not of coal-meters. And since the house was named The Coal-meter's *Arms*, it seemed clear that a coal-meter was not an instrument but a man. Coal-heavers I knew, but not coal-meters. After earnest inquiry I found that a coal-meter was distinct from a coal-heaver. He was a weigher of coal, and as Regent's Canal Dock was at one time a centre for the distribution of coal, and as each division of labour used to have its own house of call, the coal-meters no doubt used this house as a sort of club, and so induced it to change its name in their honour. Many taverns about here were used in this manner, not only as clubs but as labour bureaus and pay-offices. Even to-day, though the small employer is almost extinct, some of the few who do survive still meet their men on Friday evenings in a private room of a tavern, and settle the weekly pay-sheet in a friendly atmosphere. Another puzzling sign is that of The Bombay Grab, at Bow. This, I learn, has a story behind it. A "grab" was a particular model of sailing vessel, and it was a vessel of this model which in the eighteenth century carried to India its first import of beer, by which the India Pale Ale, so popular to-day, was created. This beer was brewed at the Bow Brewery, and by way of celebration of the event the "tap" of the brewery was given the name of The Bombay Grab.

Two interesting houses stand at opposite corners of Cable Street—The Red Lion and The Wheatsheaf. The Red Lion stands on the site of the original Red Lion inn of the eighteenth century—the house mentioned earlier as the scene of Dick Turpin's shooting, by accident, of his friend Tom King. The present house possesses a contemporary painted panel giving a spirited depiction of the incident. The interest of The Wheatsheaf lies in its war museum. Walls and ceiling are loaded with a miscellaneous collection of trophies from wars recent and long-past—shells, helmets, blunderbusses, pistols, epaulettes, swords, bugles, and all manner of military and naval mementoes. For those interested in such matters it provides a good hour's entertainment. A house of another sort of interest is The Bull's Head, in Ben Jonson Road, whose landlady, Mrs. Eliza Butterfill, has been with it these fifty years. When business is not pressing Mrs. Butterfill can tell some good stories of the East End life of the past, stories of characters and manners and customs and oddities. It stands just opposite the crowded, bazaar-like market of White Horse Street, and on a winter's night it is a pleasant little beer-house.

The Jews as a class are not much given to taverns, and there is none, I think, that could be called a Jewish resort, unless it is The Nag's Head, which is also a Jewish restaurant. There, on Friday nights, the beginning of the Sabbath, you will see many a family group; but during the week they are too busy for dalliance, and as a general rule they are more drawn to eating than to drinking. The Chinese, too, are not true tavern men, and only the more Westernized are to be seen in bars. Their favourite house seems to be The Commercial, at the corner of Pennyfields. Men of darker colour are to be seen in The Eastern Hotel and in The White Horse, Poplar High Street, and seamen and watermen everywhere. Indeed, almost any tavern about the waterside is a small East End branch of the Seven Seas Club.

Nothing about these taverns is so interesting as the stories or snatches of story that are to be overheard. Unhappily, most of these do not bear translation to the cold white page; they live only in the moment of utterance and perish like the may-fly. The setting, the company, the accent and the time are essential elements in their aptness. They have the sudden remote reality of an unintended face seen in a wall-paper or in a coal fire. On the wall or in the fire that face has a more intense life than many a face of the great canvases; cut it out of the paper, or lift it from the fire, and it is just a piece of paper or a dead coal. So with these stories. You must go there, and wait on the moment, and hear them for yourself. Ask for them at second-hand, and you will get nothing but Rosamund's Purple Jar.

MY LANDLORD, SPREAD EAGLE YARD

TAIL-PIECE

GARDINER'S CORNER at one end and The Eastern Hotel Corner at the other end make two rough Plazas for the East End. At either of these points, at any hour of the day, its varied being may be observed in little, and wherever you look from these points, over the face of the compass, you feel that you are looking to the incipient emergence of something. There, in flux and reflux, move all the factors of that being. There its moods are crystallized and the beats of its pulse may be numbered.

Down a side-street a building-site, lately razed, discloses a glimpse of the next-door garden gay with prize chrysanthemums. That is the East End.

Outside The Eastern Hotel and outside the Labour Exchanges stand groups of the unemployed—ship-repairers, boiler-makers, stevedores, navvies, leather-workers, furniture-workers, seamen. That is the East End.

At the dinner-time bright young things trimly toiletted pour into the streets from factory and warehouse. They are eager and voluble. They discuss tennis and the cinema and week-end tramps. That is the East End.

Outside a cottage a little girl is polishing the brass knocker while mother cleans the doorstep. Pride of the home; that is the East End.

Two Malays in red fez and blue suit sail along. A Rabbi in silk overcoat and tall hat shuffles along. A broken creature with a sack rakes in a dust-bin for broken scraps of food. That is the East End.

Outside the fur-dealer's stands a Sunbeam. Outside the public-house stands a Chrysler. Outside the Good Pull Up stands a Morris. Outside the little villas stand side-cars. That is the East End.

Out of the Tube comes a party of returning hoppers. They are loaded with the portable properties of the home—kettle, saucepan, frying-pan, blanket. That is the East End.

Over there is a restaurant where lunch may cost you six shillings. Outside it a stall-holder is selling basins of jellied eels at twopence, and an old woman heavily shawled trades with a large basket of begels. That is the East End.

There goes a group of Chinese; there a lonely Hindoo; there a Russian refugee; there a Balkan gipsy; there an Armenian selling silk scarves. That is the East End.

There stands a policeman looking bored to the point of inertia in his fruitless search for Crime. That is the East End.

Morning and evening groups of students, young and grown-up, books under arm, go earnestly to East London College or to Evening Classes.

That, too, and most markedly, is the East End.

* * * * *

To find one common denominator of the spirit of this conglomerate life and of the bent streets in which it breathes, is not easy. Often you think you have it, only to find on examination that it has escaped you. Melancholy you certainly perceive in its buildings and its by-ways, but melancholy is not its expression: against this melancholy is the lightness of the current Cockney. Age and weariness, too, you are sensible of, yet the motion about you is the motion of youth. My own hazard at its spirit is—something wounded but still very strong. Something that is always being battered and always coming back with new strength. Something that has lived intensely, through all distressing human experience, and is faced with yet more if anything is to be wrested from life. Ungainly, but alert. Its self-appointed seconds, in the form of busybodies with a lot of time on their hands, who are hopelessly incompetent to understand those they so blandly patronize, are for ever asking pity for it, or pestering it with the obsolete formulæ which served Arnold of Rugby. But it needs no pity, and it needs still less the fetiches of nineteenth-century bourgeoisie. It has its own strength which is lustier than anything these people, bred in only one, and that a lukewarm, style of life, have ever known.

For in this quarter, as I have said, the bulk of the sturdy and hard-up adventurers from outside make their first camp on their Dick Whittington challenge to London, and it is this quarter which supplies to the rest of London the renewal from the provinces of its ardent human stock. It may be that here, not in Bloomsbury or Mayfair or Hampstead, the true moderns are being born.

Printed in Great Britain by Butler & Tanner Ltd., Frome and London

ALSO BY THOMAS BURKE

THE FLOWER OF LIFE

New and Cheaper Issue 2s. 6d. net

"Mr. Burke's exquisite study . . . a flawless miniature."—*Liverpool Post*.

"It is to be hoped that this volume will spread the knowledge (if it still needs spreading) of how considerable a writer Mr. Burke is."—*Observer*.

"A beautiful and poignant masterpiece."—*Bookman*.

"Probably the best thing Mr. Burke has done."—*New Statesman*.

"I think it is his best."—*Sphere*.

"It is pure tragedy in a sense, but it is not a miserable or depressing book."—*Daily News*.

"A deeply moving, haunting little story."—*Tatler*.

"Beautifully rendered in lovely and musical prose."—*Referee*.

"Very simply and beautifully Mr. Burke unfolds his tragic panorama."—*Sunday Times*.

"Impossible to read without being deeply moved."—*Public Opinion*.

"Every line of his miniature drama is instinct with beauty and dignity. . . . This sorrowful and lovely book."—*Time and Tide*.

"A real contribution to literature."—*Town Crier*.

(Turn over)

ALSO BY THOMAS BURKE

CITY OF ENCOUNTERS

7s. 6d. net

"No better and finer fifty pages have been written about London than these [opening] pages of Mr. Burke's."—*Daily Telegraph.*

"I could read that sketch called 'A Pantaloon' again and again."—*Punch.*

"Here for the first time we are given a full-length sketch of Charles Chaplin which reveals as well as portrays."—*Sunday Times.*

"The study of Charles Chaplin is remarkable. Mr. Burke must have more than his normal share of the 'psychic' quality to feel the essentials of places and people as he does."—*Morning Post.*

"The long sketch of Chaplin is the most intimate description of him we have had."—*New Statesman.*

"Mr. Burke is an artist. His eye is wonderfully detective and his mind is rich with the brightest colours of expression."—*John o' London.*

"This book is wonderfully revealing. Rarely does such intimate knowledge go with such a zest for good writing."—*News-Chronicle.*

"Mr. Burke produces for us the secret magic of London; the poetry behind the poem."—*British Weekly.*

"This really lovable book. You have only to read a page or two to know that what follows will be entrancing."—*Bookman.*

ALSO BY THOMAS BURKE

THE
BOOK OF THE INN

New and Cheaper Issue 3s. 6d. net

"It was a happy thought to think of collecting word-pictures of the English inn from Chaucer's to the Dickensian masterpieces, and it has been happily carried out by Mr. Thomas Burke . . . who has done his work wisely and wittily."—*Morning Post.*

"If inn-keepers would see it, such a book as this, such a collection of recipes for merriment, is worth its weight in gold to them."—*Spectator.*

"Mr. Thomas Burke has not only done his work of selection and presentation exceedingly well, but has also written a Preface which is at once a eulogium and a justification. . . . The book should find a place in the smoke-room of every inn."—*Wine Trade Review.*

"Mr. Burke has made a great collection which betokens considerable learning."—*Manchester Guardian.*

(Turn over)

ALSO BY THOMAS BURKE

THE SUN IN SPLENDOUR
A Novel

" There is in this exciting tale vileness and squalor, greed and lust, self-seeking and, every now and then, an escape into chivalry. . . . The book is a fine one, only missing by a hair's breadth the greatness which differentiates selected from sublimated experience."—*New Statesman.*

" There is more humanity, because more reality, in *The Sun in Splendour* than in *David Copperfield.* I consider that this picture of low life is better than anything Dickens has done in that line."—A. A. B. in the *Evening Standard.*

3*s.* 6*d.* net

THE PLEASANTRIES OF OLD QUONG

" The very essence of the successful short story is embodied in these tales. The narrator's mildly delivered yet stabbing philosophy is a mental stimulant, and the reader is in turn thrilled, horrified, saddened or amused, but never, never bored."—*Evening Standard.*

" Mr. Burke is to be congratulated on the restraint and force of his new Limehouse tales. . . . He is a story-teller, born and made. He has a natural eye for situation, and a trained hand for delineation. He never wanders or fumbles. He is witty, he is a stylist. . . . Of the sixteen items in his new volume, fifteen open with a snap and go with a bang."—*Observer.*

7*s.* 6*d.* net

www.ingramcontent.com/pod-product-compliance
Lightning Source LLC
Chambersburg PA
CBHW030653230426
43665CB00011B/1077